<u>*BE!*</u>

Teta L. Jackson

BE!

by.

Teta L. Jackson

Empowering To Be, LLC
Fayetteville, NC

ISBN 978-0-578-59377-7

Empowering To Be, LLC
Fayetteville, NC
www.EmpoweringToBe.com

Dedication

This book is dedicated to my mom, Evangelist Sheryl L. Baker. Mommy, you were and will always be my best girl. I miss you terribly; and words cannot describe how much. As I think about the times we shared together I want to say thank you for leaving me with the greatest gift you could have ever given me and that is the introduction of Jesus Christ into my life. Though you are not here to read my first book, I know you saw this day afar off. Thank you for being such a wonderful example of faith and power; and thank you for showing me what trusting in our Savior really means.

This one is for you Sheryl Ann, Sheriss, Lady, Honey, Ma!
I Love You!!!

Author's Note

It is my sincere hope and desire that as you read, pray and meditate on the words within the pages of this devotional that you are inspired by my experiences and challenged through the reading of the selected verses of scripture from the Bible to **_BE!_**.

Contents

Introduction

           BE!   ix

Day One

           BE! You   12

Day Two

           BE! Purified   20

Day Three

           BE! Healed   28

Day Four

           BE! Whole   36

Day Five

           BE! Strong   44

Day Six

           BE! Bold   51

Day Seven

           BE! Sure   57

Day Eight

           BE! Empowered   64

Day Nine

           BE! Alive   71

Day Ten

           BE! Patient   78

Day Eleven

           BE! Healthy   85

Day Twelve

           BE! Forgiving   92

Day Thirteen

          BE! Faithful   99

Day Fourteen

          BE! Loving   108

Day Fifteen

          BE! Confident   115

Day Sixteen

          BE! Vigilant   122

Day Seventeen

          BE! Honest   128

Day Eighteen

          BE! Gracious   135

Day Nineteen

          BE! Fearless   141

Day Twenty

          BE! Transformed   148

Day Twenty-One

          BE! Enough   155

Day Twenty-Two

          BE! Wealthy   162

Day Twenty-Three

          BE! Kind   169

Day Twenty-Four

          BE! Encouraged   175

Day Twenty-Five

          BE! Free   182

Day Twenty-Six

          BE! Focused   189

Day Twenty-Seven

        _**BE!**_ Prayerful …………..   196

Day Twenty-Eight

        _**BE!**_ Steadfast …………..   203

Day Twenty-Nine

        _**BE!**_ Vulnerable ………....   210

Day Thirty

        _**BE!**_ Light ………………   217

Day Thirty-One

        _**BE!**_ An Experience ……..   224

About The Author ……………………   231

Thank You …………………………….   232

Introduction

BE! is a devotional written to inspire and motivate the reader to be all that God has designed them to be before the foundations of the world. The very essence of ***BE!*** is rooted in the bible and is derived from the scripture found in Jeremiah 1:5 where God tells Jeremiah "Before I formed you in the womb I knew you, before you were born I set you apart, I appointed you as a prophet to the nations." (New International Version) Here, God lays out four very important points to Jeremiah. Point one, God says "I formed you." Point two, God says "I knew you." Point three God says "I set you apart." And, Point four God says "I appointed you." Whew!! How amazing and awesome are these four phrases! God says to Jeremiah before the embryonic stage even began, before the sperm met the egg and caused you to be in existence in your mother's womb, I had already formed you, come to know who you are (your personality, quirks, idiosyncrasies), decided what I was going to set you aside to do, and made you ruler over the thing I had assigned you to. My God from Zion! God is making it clear to Jeremiah that before he was even a thought in anyone's mind to God he was already a Prophet to the nations. Jeremiah had purpose for living before he breathed the earth's air as a new born baby. He had a calling that would not and could not be changed. No matter what Jeremiah would have done, it would not have altered the fact that God had already set him apart and appointed him. God called Jeremiah

Prophet and that was the call; whether he answered to it once on earth or not, it was established.

Therefore, as it was for Jeremiah, so it is for you. Yes, you must know and be confident in the fact that you were on God's mind before your momma and daddy met. Years, months, days, hours, minutes, or seconds before you were conceived God spoke purpose over your life. He created destiny for your life that is specifically crafted for you to pursue and obtain. No one else can walk out your destiny or accomplish your God-given purpose but you. Believe that God has a plan for you and it is perfect. Know that His thoughts concerning you are perfect. Trust that His will for your life is perfect. Be assured that everything that has happened in your life is lining up perfectly and that God did not make a mistake in creating you. You are special to God and He has given you something specific and unique to accomplish. You have been formed to be someone amazing; to do something incredible. You were birthed into this world to *BE!* an answer to a need, a light in darkness, laughter to the hurting, health to the sick… You have been born for a purpose, for a work that is awaiting your arrival. It is time to walk in the BEness that lives within you, the BEness that is fighting to live out loud in the earth. It is time for you to *BE!*.

Scripture Reference

Jeremiah 1: 5 (New International Version)

Day One

BE! You

What is interesting is someone is laughing at today's proclamation to *BE!* You; while on the other hand someone is crying as a result of the very same. This simple, and yet powerful phrase is right now provoking varying reactions within the hearts and minds of each reader. It is a challenging proclamation, not because of the word "BE," but the word "You." It is not the word "BE" in and of itself that causes a powerful and sometimes paralyzing reaction within the reader. It is when the word "You" is added that the phrase takes on a meaning that can cripple the most successful sister on the planet and have her face to the ground seeking its meaning for her life. It is the words "*BE!* You" together that causes our hearts to flutter and brains to race around in our memories seeking some evidence of who this "You" is that is being spoken about. The words together are instructional and provide direction and focus on a place to which many of us have no clue. The "You" that is being proclaimed today has escaped many of us. We simply do not know who she is or where to find her. As a result, we are challenged by the thought and are uncomfortable with the idea of having to search her out. Therefore, someone may laugh and another may cry when met with the proclamation to *BE!* You. Whatever the reaction, it is likely that it is based in the train of thought which says "Be me??? That is easier said than done" or

"How do you be someone you have never known and do not know how to find??" or "How do you get back to being someone that you ran from because others told you she was not good enough???" or "How do you push past years of heartache and pain to regain the you that you sometimes see in the distance looking at you and waiting for your return" or maybe you are thinking "So much life has happened, I have reinvented myself so many times and I do not remember the authentic 'You' I am supposed To **_BE!_**." I hear your heart, but more importantly, God hears your cry.

In Psalm 139:1-4 and 13-16, the bible says:

> You have searched me, Lord, and you know me. You know when I sit and when I rise; you perceive my thoughts from afar. You discern my going out and my lying down; you are familiar with all my ways. Before a word is on my tongue you, Lord, know it completely... For you created my inmost being; you knit me together in my mother's womb. I praise you because I am fearfully and wonderfully made; your works are wonderful, I know that full well. (New International Version)

Here, David expresses to the Lord "you know me and you created me." He says that the Lord knows where he is, what he is doing and what he is about to say before it even comes off of his tongue. He continues by saying that not only does the Lord know him, but the Lord fearfully and wonderfully created him as well. David is clearly expressing that there is nothing about him that God is surprised about especially since the Lord was present with him before he was even formed in the womb. These two powerful statements when considered in the context of our Day One reading brings into perspective how the "You" that we have been speaking about has nothing to do with us and everything to do with God. It helps us to understand that as God knows us and created us, at our core, the "You" that He designed for us to be exists. There is nothing that we can do or say to alter the essence of our "You." There is no life experience that has occurred that has stomped out the plan for "You." Not even the Lord will interfere with his declared purpose and plan for "You" as stated in James 1:17 that says there is "no change or shifting with God." (Berean Study Bible) Once He declares a thing it exists. He does not take what he has said or done back, there is no variation in Him.

As a result, fear not, because you have not, cannot, will not and do not have the ability to modify the "You" that you have been created to be. It is established in the heavens and in the earth that "You" are a force to be reckoned with and that you are walking in your purpose unashamed and without hesitation. Know that your authentic and purposeful self is alive and breathing inside of you, and nothing, not even brokenness, despair, or life's failures can alter the "You" that was established before you were created. You have not been disqualified because of an act committed by you are someone else. It does not matter the issue, know that God's plan has been established for your life and the very essence of who you are is a part of your nature not your nurture. Being "You" will require very little effort once realized.

Further, understand that to discover or rediscover "You" is a process that is unique to you and your relationship with God. It is a personal journey that should be closed to the opinions and perspectives of others. It will require that you spend quality time in prayer and meditation focusing on the one who created you and knows all about you. Remember that God is the author and designer of your life. He has the blueprints and knows exactly who and what you are designed to **BE!**. He is the master builder of your life and He holds every answer to every question that you have. Trust Him to speak to you and lead and guide you as you seek to know and understand the "You" that He wills for you to **BE!**.

Prayer Starter

As you are praying and meditating today, ask God to show you "You." Ask Him to remove the blockages from your heart, mind and spirit that are preventing you from being able to clearly see "You." Ask him to strengthen you to press past the bearers and to break free of the chains that are attempting to keep you from searching out the "You" God created you to be. Ask Him to help you to _**BE!**_ You.

Scripture References

Psalm 139:1-4 and 13-16 (New International Version)
James 1:17 (Berean Study Bible)

Study Notes:

_BE!_ You

Day Two

BE! Purified

It is amazing that when the Lord started dealing with me about Day Two I immediately thought about the scripture in Job 23:10 where Job says "But He knows the way that I take [and He pays attention to it]. *When* He has tried me, I will come forth as [refined] gold [pure and luminous]." (Amplified Translation) Oh how there have been times in my life where I thought satan was moving and creating havoc only to discover that I was mistaken. I mean, what do you do when you realize that it is not satan that is tempting you, but it is God testing you? How do you pray when the one you would normally go to for help is the one that lifted the hedge of protection and is allowing chaos to access your life? Yes, we are used to rebuking and binding the enemy and we have that declaration on standby and repeat; but what happens when it is different this time. This time it is God's doing, His plan and His will. God's hand is manipulating the actors and all of the parts are being controlled by Him. There is no escape until He allows it; and all of the exit ramps are closed for repair. What do you do? This is exactly what happened in Job's life. Job was faithful to God, his family and business. He was a righteous man and had done nothing to bring the test he was experiencing into his life. Yet, God chose him to be tested anyway. This leaves us with the question, why? The simple answer is God chose him not for what Job could see about himself at that time, but for what he could not. God chose Job because he needed help in an area where he was blind. Like all of us there are blind spots in our lives that no one can see but God. These areas keep us from growing in God and becoming fully mature. As a result, with all of Job's good and upright acts, there was still something lacking and God allowed the test to help him to see himself completely.

Further, blind spots are dangerous to our spiritual growth because they hide from us our weak areas. As a result, when we are tested, we will sometimes do what Job did in Job 31, which is to stop and take inventory of our lives. How do we take inventory you ask? We stand in the presence of God and we tell Him of our marvelous works. We explain to Him how faithful we are in tithing and that we give offerings too. We exclaim of the unrighteous deeds that we did not commit and the good deeds that we have performed. We tell God how we have given to the poor, and that we feed the homeless. We say and do everything we can think of to help God understand why He may have chosen the wrong person for this test. We also make attempts to negotiate with Him by expressing all of the things we are going to do for Him if He allows the test to end; but none of this moves God. You see in our most righteous state, there is still something that needs correcting in our lives. There is still an area that we need to work on in order to be a little closer to perfection. Job found this out in Job chapters 38-41 where God declares to Job His infinite wisdom and power; and expresses to Job his lack thereof. Job had a blind spot and God chose him for testing to reveal it to him. It is in Job 42 that we discover God's purpose for testing Job. It is here that the blind spot is exposed. Job thought he knew God, he thought he was humbled; but through the test, he realized that he did not know God like he thought and that humility had actually escaped him. As a result, the test exposed areas of weakness in Job which allowed him a chance to repent.

Moreover, God's reasoning for testing Job was specific to him. Job's test was directly related to an area in his life that God in His omniscience knew needed to be fixed. And, as it was with Job, so it is with us. God knows the way that we take. He is paying close attention to us. He knows where we are falling short and what needs to be corrected before we can take that next step in our ministries, careers, and families. We aren't fooling Him at all. God loves us and wants the best for us, and sometimes the process of getting to that best does not feel good, but it is necessary. I say that it is necessary because we have to go through the test or as Job describes it, the refining fire, to come out as pure and luminous gold. The hotter the fire the more purified gold becomes. In the same respect, the hotter the fire of our test the more our blind spots are revealed giving us the opportunity to face them, deal with them and give them over to God in prayer. When I was younger, I would hear the old saints of God talking about fiery trials; it would sound so scary to me. At that time, I did not understand the true meaning of the fire. I did not know that the fire came to burn off the impurities in our lives and prepare us for the next stage of life. I could not see at that young age that the fire did not come to kill us but to make us into something better and more precious. Job received that revelation in Job 42. It is in verse 12 of Job 42 that we see God not only restore Job, but after the test, make his "latter end greater than his beginning." (New King James Version)

Therefore, we must understand that this is the will of God for our lives. He wants us to **BE!** Purified. God wants us to go through the test knowing that it is His will for us to be better than we were before the fire. Do not run away from the test. Walk boldly through it having faith that if God brought you to it He will bring you safely through it. Open your heart while you are going through. Do not say why me God, but say here I am God. What do I need to learn through this test? I am your servant speak to me that I might be purified.

I remember going through one of the worst times of my life as a Christian. It was one of the most painful seasons I have ever endured! At one of my lowest points in that season I went to my Pastor in total disbelief and I asked him with an anguished voice and tears running down my face "Why is this happening to me?" And, without hesitation he said, "It's not happening to you, it's happening for you." I understand his statement now more than ever today. Let the test happen for you. You will be better for it in the end.

Prayer Starter

As you are praying and meditating today, ask God to reveal your blind spots. Ask Him to sensitize your spirit that you will be able to discern when He is speaking. Ask Him to give you ears to hear and a heart to know and understand His voice. Ask God to give you the ability to endure the fiery tests knowing that you will come out as refined and purified gold. Ask God to help you remember that the test is not happening to you, but it is indeed happening for you. Ask God to help you to stand through the process that you may _**BE!**_ Purified.

Scripture References

Job 23:10 (Amplified Translation)
Job 38-41
Job 42:12 (New King James Version)

_BE!_ Purified

_____
_____
_____
_____
_____
_____
_____
_____
_____
_____
_____
_____
_____
_____
_____
_____
_____
_____
_____
_____
_____
_____
_____
_____
_____
_____
_____
_____
_____
_____
_____
_____
_____
_____
_____
_____
_____
_____
_____

Day Three

BE! Healed

Many years ago, actually in 1992, I was asked to speak at a women's conference my church was hosting. I was extremely excited about the opportunity, but I was nervous as well. Although this was early in my years of being in ministry, I understood that what I was being asked to do was of high importance. Yes, it was an honor to be trusted with the privilege of delivering the word of God; but it was also a responsibility that I did not want to take lightly. Therefore, I began to pray immediately asking God what He wanted the congregation to hear from Him through me. Not long after I began to seek God for direction I had a dream. This dream was like none other I had ever had and it rattled me at the very core of my being.

In the dream, I lived in a house that was actually my mind. As I walked around my house, which again represented my mind, I saw spider webs everywhere. Spider webs went from the ceiling to floors, from wall to wall and room to room. They were everywhere! As I continued to walk through the house I began to notice something different about the webs. I noticed that instead of them being soft as they normally are they were hard like glass. As odd as that was I also noticed that though there were webs everywhere I did not immediately see any spiders. As I was walking around the house trying to understand what was happening I raised my head to the ceiling where there was a lone light fixture; and in the center of the light fixture I saw one spider. In that moment I instantly knew that this one spider had weaved all of the webs in the house. As soon as I came to that conclusion every web in the house began to crumble as if someone had shattered a glass. As the webs were crumbling around me I began to cry out to God, "Lord my mind is crumbling, my mind is crumbling." Instantly I woke up from the dream, but when I woke up something woke up with me; and that something was memories of incidents that happened to me as a child that I had pushed into the deepest part of my mind. These were memories that had been sleeping for years and eating away at my mind waiting for the right time to shatter my future. These were memories that I literally had "forgotten" and in that moment wished that I could forget them again.

These memories brought with them emotional pain that I had never experienced. I woke up from the dream in tears. I was in anguish! The memories were overwhelming and I didn't know what to do with them and I didn't know how to handle what I was feeling; but in the midst of my tears and confused state I heard God say, "Kill the Spider: Deal with your Past Before It Destroys Your Present and Your Future." In that moment, it became clear to me that as uncomfortable as it was for me to be reminded of some of the worst times in my life I had to face my past head-on. I could no longer hide from the pain. I had to deal with it for the sake of my sanity and for the sake of my future. The message that God gave me from the dream is the message that He used me to deliver to the women in 1992. It was a message of emotional healing; and it is the message that I give to you in our Day Three devotional. ***BE!*** Healed, kill your spider. Don't let the pain of your past destroy your now and your tomorrow.

One of my most favorite scriptures is Isaiah 53:5, which says "But he was wounded for our transgressions, he was bruised for our iniquities; the chastisement of our peace was upon him; and with his stripes we are healed." (New King James Version) In the New Testament, I Peter 2:24 follows in the same vain reading "...By whose stripes we were healed." (New King James Version) Isaiah says that "we are healed" and I Peter says "we were healed." I love putting both scriptures together side by side because it helps us to know that we are either healed right now in this moment or we have been healed at some other point in time. Either way, healing belongs to us as God's people; and this healing is not limited to physical healing, but it applies to any and all healing that we need and that includes emotional healing as well.

Many of us are carrying pain from our past and we are afraid to speak it out or share it with anyone. We are holding on to it like we are protecting the greatest secret known to humankind; and to us the secret is just that big. We are doing what we were told as children "we don't take the family business out of the house." We are holding on to these secrets for dear life not realizing that they are killing us softly from the inside out. It is imperative that the ugliness of yesterday really becomes the ugliness of yesterday. God is declaring that today he wants us to ***BE!*** Healed.

God's ability to heal us can manifest in several different ways. He can heal us instantly by divine intervention and he can also use medical professionals to assist us in obtaining our healing. Both ways are great because they both need God's power and might to be successful. Either way the healing comes is awesome. The key here is that we recognize that there is an ailment and we open ourselves to receive the manifestation of healing in our lives.

Further, I read a lot of books as I was working towards total and complete emotional healing. I read the bible and I also read books that dealt directly with my situation. Do whatever you have to do to ensure that you are not held in emotional bondage to something from your past; do not give that issue control over your life any longer. Stop pushing it down or pretending that it does not exist. Do not prolong the healing process any longer. Face what has happened and get past it that you might move forward into your next chapter free of any past pains or disappointments. Healing belongs to us. Not because I said it, but because God has declared it to be for our lives.

Prayer Starter

As you are praying and meditating today, ask God to reveal to you any hidden areas in your life that may be killing you mentally and emotionally. Ask Him to give you the strength that you need to face that issue, admit that the issue happened, give it to God, get counseling if you need to and then move forward. Ask God to cover you through your process of emotional healing and reveal to you the right person to share your "secret" with if necessary. Ask God to be with you as you walk out His will for you to ***BE!*** Healed.

Scripture References

Isaiah 53:5 (New King James Version)
I Peter 2:24 (New King James Version)

__BE!__ Healed

_____
_____
_____
_____
_____
_____
_____
_____
_____
_____
_____
_____
_____
_____
_____
_____
_____
_____
_____
_____
_____
_____
_____
_____
_____
_____
_____
_____
_____
_____

Day Four

BE! Whole

When I think about the word "whole" I see parts that were once separated being put back together again. I see fragmented pieces coming together to form the thing that it was intended to represent all along. To me the word "whole" speaks of strength and unity. Therefore, when the phrase *BE!* Whole is read aloud it becomes a declaration in the earth that says division no longer exists; and that every individual part has now linked together as one to form a collective that is stronger than what any of its individual parts would ever be alone. As a result, being whole is not an option for success in life; it is essential. When a person is whole they are complete within themselves and they are lacking nothing. This idea of wholeness applies to every part of our lives including our spirits, souls and bodies.

In considering the proclamation *BE!* Whole, Mark 5:25-34 comes to my mind. In this bible story, we find a woman who has been sick for twelve years with what is described as "an issue of blood." This means that she had a continuous flow that may have been as a result of hemorrhaging or some other blood disease. She had been suffering for a long time and when we find her in the scriptures she is at a place of desperation. I use the word desperation because not only is she dealing with her blood issue, but she is also experiencing financial lack as well. We know this

36

because according to Mark 5:26 she spent all of her money on physicians in hopes of finding a cure for her issue but none of them could heal her, and as matter of fact she became worse. Additionally, I believe the woman is at a place of desperation because she is faced with social issues and stigma established in Jewish culture which deems her unclean and requires that she be ostracized as a result of her issue. This means that if she was married, if she had children, if she was involved in any social clubs, or participated in any other activities, she was no longer allowed to have contact with her family or do any of the things that were familiar to her. Essentially, this issue of blood had her sick in her body, financially destitute and alone. The issue caused division between her and all of the support systems that existed in her life. As a result where she was once fortified and strengthened by other people and activities, she was now forced to handle the issue on her own. She was forced into a position where she had to do something different because she had to get something different. Sounds like desperation to me. As the story continues, in Mark 5:29, when all else had failed, she heard of Jesus, and as he was passing in a crowd, she reached out and touched His garment, "the fountain of her blood was dried up" and she was healed. (King James Version)

This is such a powerful story of faith; and it is from the perspective of having faith in God that many speak when discussing these verses and that is right to do; but there is more here to unpack. Yes, the woman exercised faith and received healing for her physical body, but that was only one-third of the problem that she was facing. When she touched Jesus's garment, she was also experiencing financial and social problems as well. For Jesus to heal one part of her life and leave the other parts unaddressed would not represent a complete healing for the woman. He had to address all aspects of her life and that is exactly what He did. In Mark 5:34 Jesus shows us that he cares about us totally and completely. Jesus says "Daughter, thy faith hath made thee whole; go in peace, and be whole of thy plague." (King James Version) Now the first use of the word "whole" in Mark 5:34 in the Greek means saved; but the second word "whole" is a literal translation. The second word literally means to "be whole." Jesus is saying to the woman, every part of your life that has been fragmented as a result of your issue **_BE!_** Whole, come back together as one unit and operate once again in wholeness. We must understand that Jesus recognized that the woman was healed physically before He said anything to her, which is why he said "who touched me" in Mark 5:31. Therefore, he was not only addressing her physical condition when he said "be whole; but He was referencing every aspect of her life. When Jesus began to speak to the woman in verse 34 He was speaking to all of the areas that were forced out of place and alignment as a result of her issue. Jesus was saying daughter now that you are healed physically let your finances come back together again. Now that you are healed physically, let your marriage and family relationships come back together again. Now that you are healed physically let your social gatherings commence again.

For this reason, just as Jesus spoke to the woman who had the issue of blood, I come into agreement with you that not only will you be healed physically, but you will **_BE!_** Whole in every area of your life as well. I agree with you that all of the parts that make up who you are will come together in unity and flow exactly how they were designed to before any issue touched your life. I believe with you that not only will you be completely healed from your issue, but that the money loss you suffered as a result of the issue will be restored back to you. I agree with you that your family will smile again. I believe that laughter will fill the empty spaces of your home and that your social calendar will be full again. I stand with you in agreement that everything that you loved to do before the issue that you will do it again with great passion. I agree that you will be strengthened once again and that you will live a full and meaningful life without stress, worry or shame. I believe and agree with you that you will not be healed only but you will **_BE!_** Whole.

Prayer Starter

As you are praying and meditating today, ask God to heal your issue. Believe Him for the healing and trust him for the manifestation. Ask God to restore back to you everything that you lost as a result of the issue. Ask Him to return back to you your smile, your home, your lifestyle and any other thing that was affected by the issue. Ask Him to restore the joy in your marriage and other family relationships. Tell God that you do not want to be healed of your issue only but that you want to **_BE!_** Whole.

Scripture Reference

Mark 5: 25-34 (King James Version)

Study Notes:

_BE!_ Whole

Day Five

BE! Strong

    BE! Strong… Have you ever gone through a challenge in your life and someone told you to "Be Strong?" It is a very interesting thing to say to a person especially in times of disappointment, despair and heartache; but it is in those times that the phrase seems to be used the most. You lost your job? Be strong. You lost your loved one? Be strong. You are sick? Be strong. You feel hopeless and you do not know which way to go? Be strong. It is as if the phrase has taken on a life of its own and is now the go to phrase when it comes to encouraging someone who is at a low place in life. It is a phrase that has been said to me, but it is also a phrase that I have said to others as well. The phrase is meant to provide comfort to the person who is experiencing hard times. The purpose behind the phrase is to remind the person that no matter what is going on right now, be who you already are, and that is strong. When considering the phrase in this light I completely understand why it is used; but the question some may have is how is strength derived when a person is at the weakest point in their lives? How does one become strong when all hope seems to be lost?

    One of the things I love about being a Christian is that I know I am never alone in this life. Even when I feel that I am at a lonely place, I can rest assured that I am not by myself because according to Deuteronomy 31:6 God will "never leave [me] or forsake [me]." This scripture in itself brings comfort to me that no matter what I am experiencing God is always there. We are never in it by ourselves; and as this is truth, even at our weakest moments God is right there with us. He is there to comfort us, guide us, provide for us and strengthen us. God knew that there would be times in our lives where we would not have enough strength to keep going or to fight. He knew that within ourselves we would not be able to push past the disappointments of life to obtain victory over our trails and tests. Therefore, He gives us nuggets of hope throughout the bible to let us know He is right there with us. This is comforting to know. He does not want us to try to be strong on our own because the truth of the matter is we cannot do it in our own strength. This is why He says to us through the Apostle Paul in Ephesians 6:10 "Finally, my bretheren, be strong in the Lord, and in the power of his might." (New King James Version) God knew that when we were up against incredible battles that fighting in our strength would not be sufficient. He knew that we would need more power than what we would be able to muster on our own. He knew that we would need His strength.

As Christians, there is no other way for us to become spiritually fortified and strengthened except through God; and His word is the vehicle by which we obtain our strength. As a result, when taking closer inspection of the word "strong" in Ephesians 6:10 we see that it is defined as "to make strong or to enable." In other words the word strong implies that the Lord makes us strong or enables us to be strong. Moreover, the word strong is defined as

"I empower, fill with power, or strengthen." In addition, the words power and might in Ephesians 6:10 both mean strength. Therefore, as we have dissected the verse as described herein, when reassembled, the verse is saying *"The Lord makes us strong or enables us to be strong, as a result be empowered, filled with power, strengthened in Him, and in His strength and of His strength."* My God today! Nowhere in Ephesians 6:10 is God requiring us to be strong in and of ourselves. The entire verse is pointing us to God and the strength that lies within Him, not in us. The command for us to **BE!** Strong is entirely based in our ability to recognize and accept the strength of the Lord as our own and operate from that position of strength alone.

It is very humbling to know that God has thought about every aspect of our lives. He loves us and He knew that we would have problems and experience situations that would be too much for us to handle on our own. For this reason he tells us to **BE!** Strong; but, his expectation is not that we are strong in our own strength, but in His. This means that no matter what we may be facing in life God has enough strength for each of us. All we have to do is take on his strength for our battles may be too much for us to stand, but in Him we "can do all things as He gives us the strength." (Philippians 4:13, King James Version) **BE!** Strong in the Lord because He is our strength.

Prayer Starter

As you are praying and meditating today, ask God to help you to know you are not alone. Ask Him to cover you in His strength, and make His presence known to you. Ask Him to help you to recognize that His strength is made perfect in your weakness." (2 Corinthians 12:9, King James Version) Ask Him to help you to **_BE!_** Strong in Him.

Scripture References

Deuteronomy 31:6
Ephesians 6:10 (King James Version)
Philippians 4:13 (King James Version)
2 Corinthians 12:9 (King James Version)

_BE!_ Strong

Day Six

BE! Bold

When I think about being bold I think about the relationship that children have with their parents. I think about the child who knows without any doubt that their mother owns a bank and has access to unlimited wealth. As a result, the child will approach mom with boldness requesting that mom buy any and everything the child wants taking no regard for the cost of the item or any other financial responsibility that mom may have. Children in their innocence and naivety expect that their parents have the ability to fix every problem, provide for every need and handle every issue that may arise in their lives. Therefore, when a child approaches their parent, it is typically with the expectation that whatever has to be done mom will make sure that it is handled. That is why when someone does something to a child, the first thing they will say is "I'm going to tell my mom." In the child's mind mom will work the situation out for them so everybody better watch out! Although this may be annoying for many parents, it is actually the perfect picture of what our relationship should be like with our Father and God in heaven.

As a Christian, we are supposed to be comfortable enough in our relationship with God that we can come to Him with any need or any situation and receive help from Him. This is exactly what the author of the book of Hebrews expressed to us in Hebrews 4:15-16.

The verses read "For we have not a high priest which cannot be touched with the feeling of our infirmities; but was in all points tempted like as we are, yet without sin. Let us therefore come boldly unto the throne of grace that we may obtain mercy, and find grace to help in time of need." (King James Version) Here, the scripture is clear, there is nothing that we cannot come boldly to God about. Nothing! As a matter of fact the verses provide that Jesus, as our high priest, experienced the same feelings that we have in our everyday lives. He understands what we are going through and He sits on the throne ready to receive us with mercy and grace to help us in our time of need.

The picture that is painted for us as children of God in Hebrews 4:15-16 is beyond beautiful. Not only is the empathy of our savior expressed here, but mercy and grace is extended to us as well. In these scriptures God is saying there is no judgment for us in His presence. He is saying for us to come to Him boldly and without fear or hesitation. He says come to Him and receive the mercy and grace that we need. God is here for us. He wants to help us in whatever state we may find ourselves. There is no situation that is too difficult for Him or problem that He will not be able to help us resolve. There is no issue or sin that we are dealing with that will cause God to turn his back on us or reject us because of.

This is the good news of the Gospel. This is good news for our lives. God loves us. We are His children and He is here for us. All we have to do is **_BE!_** Bold in our approach to Him. We do not have to enter into His presence with our heads held down because

52

He is not condemning us. His arms are open wide for us; and according to John 16:23 we can come to Him asking anything in the name of Jesus and He shall give it to us.

Therefore, the question today is what has been keeping us from going to God? What has made us feel like our lives are too messed up to boldly step into His presence and seek His help? Remember that there is no sin that is too much for our Father to handle. There is nothing or no one that can stop us from coming to Him for help, but us. *BE!* Bold today! Step into the presence of God without fear or shame. Lay everything at his feet, no matter how ugly you may think it is. Take it to God and let Him handle it. Mercy and grace are waiting for you. Today is your day to *BE!* Bold.

Prayer Starter

As you are praying and meditating today, ask God to help you to see Him as your father and not as your judge. Ask Him to help you with your situation. Ask Him to shower you with mercy and grace. Ask Him to let His love pour over you like rain. Ask him to help you to *BE!* Bold.

Scripture References

Hebrews 4:15-16 (King James Version)
John 16:23

Study Notes:

_BE!_ Bold

_____
_____
_____
_____
_____
_____
_____
_____
_____
_____
_____
_____
_____
_____
_____
_____
_____
_____
_____
_____
_____
_____
_____
_____
_____
_____
_____
_____
_____
_____
_____
_____

Day Seven

BE! Sure

I am of the strong belief that there is absolutely nothing that I can do without God. As a result, I am always checking in with Him to make sure nothing has changed. I have learned some very hard lessons in life; and one of those lessons is to stay in tune with God always because things change. Now listen, I did not say that God changes, I said things change or the way by which we are to accomplish something may change. Therefore, I have found it to be very important to make sure that I am always where I am supposed to be, doing exactly what I am supposed to be doing according to the plan of God for my life. One way that I accomplish this is by asking God to sensitize my spirit that I know when He is moving and that I know when something has shifted. I never want to be in a situation where I am on an Island and realize that I am there without God. I will be alright if I am on an Island with Him, but without Him, no thank you! I need the hand of God to be evident in my life at all times. My sincerest prayer is that I walk the path that He has designed and not the one that I have created. I know God has a destiny and purpose for me; and He has destiny and purpose for you as well.

With that being said, as I was considering our devotional for today the verse of scripture that came to my mind is Philippians 1:6 that says "Be sure of this one thing, that he who has begun a good work in you shall perform it until the day of Jesus Christ." (English Standard Version) When I began writing the devotional for this day my focus was on **me** making sure that **I** was in line with the plan of God; but, as I meditated on this verse something changed. My focus went from what I was doing to ensure that I did not break my promise to God to what He is doing to ensure that He keeps His promise to me. No longer was I considering my own acts and commitment to God, but I was now in awe of His dedication to me.

As I studied the scripture, I recognized that it is God that is doing the work, and we are on the receiving end of His efforts. The verse says that we need to ***BE!*** Sure or confident of one thing only and that is as God has started something good in us He shall without a doubt make sure that it is completed until Jesus comes again. This is such a wonderful perspective on our relationship with God. We serve a God who is concerned about all aspects of our lives; and He wants everything that has been designed for our lives to manifest not just once in our lifetime, but continuously until we meet Jesus Christ at our end. This scripture is incredibly encouraging because many of us think that God has a "you're disqualified" button that He is waiting to push whenever we make a mistake or fall off track. We think that the thing we did last night or the words we spoke today made God say that we are not good enough or someone else is a better choice for the blessing. Well, let me tell you something, Philippians 1:6 says otherwise.

There is nothing that we can do to change the plan of God for our lives. We have to know that it is God who started the good work in us and it is God who will ensure its completion. As Jeremiah 1:12 says God is watching over His word until it is fulfilled. He will not take His eyes off of us until who He has called us to be, what He has called us to do and where He has called us to go has manifested. God is own assignment; He is at work in our lives. The only obligation we have is to **_BE!_** Sure that He will do exactly what He said He will for us. We have to know that God is not like man. He cannot lie. Once He speaks something it shall happen. As Isaiah 55:11 says "… my word that goes out from my mouth: It will not return to me empty, but will accomplish what I desire and achieve the purpose for which I sent it." (New International Version) God wants every good word that He has said about us to be manifested on the earth; and He wants it to be manifested over and over and over again until we meet our end. As much as we may want to see ourselves operating within His plan, we must know that He wants to see it more; and of this we must **_BE!_** Sure.

Prayer Starter

As you are praying and meditating today, ask God to help you to know His will for your life. Ask Him to help you to be sensitive to His move in your life. Ask God to help you to **_BE!_** Sure of His ability to complete the good work that He has started in you. Ask God to manifest that good work in your life continuously until Jesus returns.

Scripture References

Philippians 1:6 (English Standard Version)
Jeremiah 1:12
Isaiah 55:11 (New International Version)

Study Notes:

_**BE!**_ Sure

Day Eight

BE! Empowered

Being patient and waiting for something to happen is difficult for many of us to do. It is especially hard for us as we live in a society where a faster way to accomplish something is produced every day. It seems like daily we are presented with a quicker way to prepare food, loss weight, drive to our destination, and so much more. The idea that says who has time to wait when we can accomplish what we need to have performed in a matter of seconds instead of hours is prevalent; and I understand. Why wait when we can have what we want and need now? With the invention of products like the microwave, pressure cooker and air fryer we have gained precious hours in our week that can now be dedicated to other projects. In addition, grocery stores now have applications where we can order our groceries and someone will deliver them to us at the designated curbside or inside pick-up section of the store or we even have the option of them being delivered directly to our homes. Although these products and applications may be developed with the purpose of helping us save time and create opportunity, we must be mindful that we not allow that same idea to create within us an inability or unwillingness to wait for the manifestation of the spiritual in our lives. We must make sure that we are not in a hurry to move from one spiritual experience to another experience. Waiting for God to speak or guide is important. If we move too fast we may miss out on our opportunity to *BE!* Empowered.

I believe this is what Jesus was saying to the disciples before He ascended to the Father. In Luke 24:49, the verse says "… I am sending you what my Father promised. As for you, stay in the city until you are empowered from on high." (Christian Standard Bible) In Acts 1:8 the story is told again from the perspective of another writer. The verse reads, "But you will receive power when the Holy Spirit has come upon you; and you will be my witnesses both in Jerusalem, and in all Judea and Samaria, and even the remotest parts of the earth." (New American Standard Version) In both versions of the story, Jesus told the disciples who had been with Him for three years to remain in the city where they were because they needed to be empowered. Jesus was saying to the disciples though you have seen me do great works and have had extraordinary spiritual experiences with me there is something else that you need before you move forward in the next phase of ministry; and that is to ***BE!*** Empowered.

It is important for us to note here that we must ***BE!*** Empowered by God before stepping into what is next for our lives. The word empowered has several definitions. Two of the definitions that stand out to me are authorized and licensed. When Jesus told the disciples to stay where they were until they were empowered, He was saying to them to wait to receive actual power and strength; but He was also saying to them to wait for their authorization or license to act. Jesus was essentially saying, do not preach, teach, pray, lay hands, or be a witness about Him until they received authorization or license to proceed. This is interesting because one would think that the disciples would have been prepared and could have launched directly into ministry upon the ascension of Jesus to the Father; but this was not the case. Their spiritual experiences with Jesus were not enough to qualify them for the next phase of ministry. Something additional was required which meant that they had to spend more time waiting on their current level before moving to the next.

Moreover, making sure that we have received everything that we need on our current level is extremely important because it is the current level that will prepare us for the next phase in our lives. Having to wait when we feel we are prepared for the next phase can be difficult and discouraging as well; but, going to the next level prematurely may expose weakness and flaws that waiting may resolve. Take the lead of the disciples and wait to receive everything that you need on your current level. Do not be anxious about moving to the next phase of life. Wait patiently and *__BE!__* Empowered by God before stepping into what is next.

Prayer Starter

As you are praying and meditating today, ask God to help you to understand that you are waiting for a purpose. Ask Him to reveal that purpose to you while you are waiting. Ask Him to help you understand that prior spiritual experiences alone do not always qualify you for the next level. Ask Him to speak to your heart while you are waiting to *__BE!__* Empowered by Him.

Scripture References

Luke 24:49 (Christian Standard Bible)
Acts 1:8 (New American Standard Version)

BE! Empowered

Day Nine

BE! Alive

There are so many days, probably more than I can remember where I woke up feeling like the world had gotten the best of me and I was on the losing side of the fight. When I was laid off from my job, experienced a miscarriage, went through a divorce and lost my home and car – more than once, I thought there was no way life could hit me any harder than it already had; but how wrong was I to assume that as fact. It was not until my mom passed away that I was knocked off of my feet and the referee started counting down from ten. When I "lost" my mom everything seemed to be different. I did not sleep, eat, think or even breathe the same. I literally felt like I was living the life of the undead because I was physically alive but I was cold on the inside. Although all of my activities were the same after she passed, something was different. I went to work, I met friends for lunch, I talked to family on the phone, and performed household chores but I was not the same. I was walking around in the suit that was me but I was not really there. My body was present and accounted for but my heart was cold and iced over. The blood that should have been running through my veins appeared as if it had stopped. I was no longer living life but I was simply surviving from day-to-day. I was experiencing what I have now termed as *The Dracula Effect.* I was cold and lifeless on the inside but to the outside world I was alive and well. I had been hit hard. I was dazed and confused; and finding my way back to where I was prior to my mom passing seemed to be a virtual impossibility. Over time, as I prayed to God about my pain and heartache, I begin to realize that something was changing inside of me. As I consistently meditated on bible verses I began to tell myself that though tests, trials, heartaches and disappointments negatively impact our lives they are a part of what makes us mature into our predesigned purpose. As a result, it is our responsibility to make sure that we do not allow them to steal from us our opportunity to **_BE!_** Alive and receive the best that God has for us.

In the same vein, we are reminded of this truth when we read John 10:10. Jesus says "The thief does not come except to steal, and to kill, and to destroy. I have come that they may have life, and that they may have *it* more abundantly." (King James Version) Many of us are right now in a place where the thief is trying to steal, kill and destroy us. Some of us have recognized who or what the thief is in our lives and some have not; but either way we must understand that the thief is at work. The thief of chaos in the family unit, confusion on the job, financial problems, physical and mental health sicknesses, over eating, laziness, procrastination, and more is at work in our lives trying to prevent us from obtaining the abundant life that Jesus says is ours.

Further, as we dissect John 10:10, note that the word life means Zoë or the life of God; and the word abundant is translated to mean beyond measure. Therefore, with this understanding let us look at the verse again. Here, Jesus is saying that He came because

He wants us to have the *kind of life that God has until we no longer have the ability to measure the extent of God's life within us*. Consider that for a minute. Jesus is saying to us that whatever life God has we can have; but not only can we have this life, but we can have it beyond what can be measured or calculated. In other words, He is saying we can have the life of God until it overflows in our lives and saturates all of the areas that are contrary to His purpose. This is amazing news!

As a result, for those of us that have found ourselves in a place of deep depression, incredible sickness, hopelessness, despair, financial need or who are experiencing enormous heartache God wants us to take on His abundant and immeasurable life. The enemy is on assignment and ready to strike at any moment; but the word of God has come to us to declare that we have the right to ***BE!*** Alive in Jesus and of this we must be assured. There is nothing that the enemy can do to prevent us from walking in this revelation. Healing is ours because it is declared for us by God in Isaiah 53:5. Financial increase is ours because our Father owns cattle on thousands of hills according to Psalm 50:10. Sound mental health is ours because God says he will keep us in perfect peace whose mind is stayed on Him as found in Isaiah 26:3. The life that God has is the life that Jesus declared is ours – immeasurably. All we have to do is receive what we need from Him.

Prayer Starter

As you are praying and meditating today, ask God to touch your heart and cause the blood to circulate through your veins again. Ask Him to identify in you any areas where the enemy is attempting to steal, kill and destroy in your life. Ask Him to let His abundant life manifest in you until there is no way to measure it or calculate it in your life. Tell God who and what you are according to His word – healed, delivered, set-free from bondage, experiencing wealth untold. Ask Him to help you to ***BE!*** Alive.

Scripture References

John 10:10 (King James Version)
Isaiah 53:5 and 26:3
Psalm 50:10

__BE!__ Alive

_____
_____
_____
_____
_____
_____
_____
_____
_____
_____
_____
_____
_____
_____
_____
_____
_____
_____
_____
_____
_____
_____
_____
_____
_____
_____
_____
_____
_____
_____
_____
_____
_____
_____
_____

Day Ten

BE! Patient

If I am honest, when things are not going the way that I want them to go and it is taking a lot longer than I hoped for something to transpire the last thing I want to hear from a well-meaning friend or family member is to ***BE!*** Patient. It may be exactly what I need to hear, and exactly what I need to do; but it is certainly not what I want to do in the moment. The reasoning behind me or probably many people not wanting to receive the sound advice of being patient is a simple one. The idea of being patient rests in the fact that we do not know when the thing we desire to happen will actually manifest which means the call for us to exercise patience also comes with a requirement to have faith. You see when we turn everything that we have done in our own strength over to this idea of patience we are giving up control to the unknown. We are releasing our grip off it, giving it to God and trusting that it will come to pass when it is time; and this is the definition of faith. In Hebrews 11:1 the bible says "Now faith is the substance of things hoped for, the evidence of things not seen." (King James Version) Here, the verse is saying that faith is our assurance, substance and evidence that what we are praying and believing God for is going to happen. In other words, faith is the only proof we need that it will manifest. Therefore, when exercising patience, we are not leaning on our ability at all, but we are trusting in God by faith that what He has given to us will be fulfilled.

78

As a matter of fact, the author of the book of James confirms for us this idea of patience in James 1:4 where the bible says "But let patience have *its* perfect work, that you may be perfect and complete, lacking nothing." (New King James Version) Consider the word "let" in the first part of the verse. As defined, "let" means to allow, permit or give permission to. The word presents options in that the party to which it is directed has a choice to do the opposite and deny permissions as well. This means that we can either "let" patience work in us or we can deny patience the opportunity to do its job. We can chose to handle things on our own or we can take our hands off of it and have faith that as we exercise patience everything will work out the way it is supposed to in the end.

Further, as we put James 1:4 into context, chapter 1 begins with the writer encouraging other believers in Jesus Christ as they are going through trials and their faith is being tested. The writer says in James 1:2-3, "My brethren, count it all joy when ye fall into divers temptations; knowing *this*, that the trying of your faith worketh patience." (King James Version) It is in verse 4 that the writer follows with "But, let patience have *its* perfect work." The author is saying that when our faith is tested and we go through trials patience is produced. Therefore, we should let patience perform a perfect and complete work within us that we not lack for anything or in anyway. Here, the verse is saying that we should simply **_BE!_** Patient; not for patience sake alone, but because God wants to perform a perfect and complete work in us that we might be full in every area of our lives. As a result, when we pray concerning

79

patience, the prayer is not to ask God to give us patience as in doing so we are really asking him to bring test and trail into our lives; but we should **_BE!_** Patient and pray that God will perfect and complete a work in us where we are lacking absolutely nothing.

As I stated earlier, I totally understand wanting to have "it" now. I know that waiting is difficult and it may cause issues that may negatively impact us as a result; but, exercising patience is necessary to ensure that we are not making life altering mistakes. If we take our time and allow patience to do its job within us we may ultimately avoid a lot of heartache and disappointment. When we have not received what we need or know God has promised to us we should walk in what the scriptures have established and **_BE!_** Patient. It will manifest in time and it will be complete lacking nothing.

Prayer Starter

As you are praying and meditating today, ask God to give you the strength to release control and allow Him to take over. Ask Him to help you identify and overcome the fear or anxiety you may be caring and guide you as you walk in faith trusting Him for the right outcome. Ask God, as you let patience have its perfect work in you to cause you to be perfect and complete lacking nothing. Declare in prayer that you will **_BE!_** Patient knowing that everything is ultimately working for your good even if you cannot see it right now.

Scripture References

Hebrews 11:1 (King James Version)
James 1:4 (New King James Version)
James 1:1-3 (King James Version)

__BE!__ Patient

_____
_____
_____
_____
_____
_____
_____
_____
_____
_____
_____
_____
_____
_____
_____
_____
_____
_____
_____
_____
_____
_____
_____
_____
_____
_____
_____
_____
_____
_____
_____
_____
_____
_____

Day Eleven

BE! Healthy

Somebody just read the devotional topic for today and said "*BE!* Healthy... Oh, she's meddling now." Ha! Well, that is right. I am meddling; not because I want to mind other people's business, but because I want each of us to be around for many years to come that we might be healthy enough to mind our own business. I want us to live a life where our survival is not connected to prescription medicine and medical machines. I want us to live a life where we eat to live and not live to eat. I want us to enjoy the food that we eat, but not be addicted to it at the same time. I want us to stop allowing the food that we eat to kill us softly with each bite. I want us to love ourselves enough that we choose life over eating the wrong foods, overeating or not eating enough. I want us to stop getting sick and dying of illnesses that could have been prevented if we had made different food choices. As a matter of fact, I am declaring right now that "No premature death shall come upon anyone that is reading this devotional today." Today is the day that we turn away from our bad habits and incorporate new ones that represent our desire to do and be better in the area of food consumption. Today is the day that we make the decision to *BE!* Healthy and live long and purposeful lives in the name of Jesus.

It is interesting that in the church world we spend a lot of time discussing the regeneration of souls and proclaiming that our souls must be saved; but there are very few messages designed to teach us how to maintain or transform into healthy physical beings. There are messages preached around the world regarding evangelizing souls for Christ; but, when it comes to discussing our health the conversations seem to be few and far in between. As someone who grew up in church I may have heard a pastor preach on the topic of eating and food choices maybe twice in my lifetime and I may be stretching it a bit. As a result, I have often wondered why the topic of physical health is not discussed as much as other topics in our local churches. I personally would like the topic to fall within the top three lessons that my pastor teaches. It can be right at the top of the pastoral preaching list as follows and in no particular order: soul salvation, financial prosperity and good health. My reasons are simple (a) our souls being saved is a critical piece to evangelizing the world for Christ, (b) we will most certainly need money to carry out the works involved with evangelizing, and (c) sickness hinders our ability to operate effectively in the things of God, therefore we must **_BE!_** Healthy.

The bible addresses the issue of health when Apostle John sent a letter to his friend Gaius in 3 John 1:2. John says "Beloved, I pray that in all respects you may prosper and be in good health, just as your soul prospers." (New American Standard Bible) John is saying to Gaius that he first of all wants him to prosper in everything and everyway. He then says in addition to being prosperous in all things, he wants Gaius to be in good health; and he wants both of these things to occur in the same way that Gaius' soul is prospering.

86

In short, John is saying that as much as the soul or spiritual part of Gaius is prospering he also wants the same prosperity for Gaius in the area of his health. John tells Gaius that his faithful service to the church and the love that he is expressing is needed and appreciated, but in saying all of that, take care of your health because being in good health will enable you to continue to perform your God-given assignment.

It is not wise for us to do more to care for our soul than we do for the physical body that the soul lives within. We must remember that our bodies are the temple where the Holy Spirit dwells. We are carrying precious cargo and should therefore treat our bodies with the love and care that it most certainly deserves. Therefore, eating right and exercising should be a constant in our lives. We must make a commitment to ourselves to choose us first. We can join a gym, hire a trainer, or nutritionist; but whatever we do we should develop a plan that will produce a healthy lifestyle for us. God is using John and Gaius today to show us ourselves. He is saying to us that as we are in the church working for the Lord, we have a responsibility to ourselves to **_BE!_** Healthy in our physical bodies as well.

Prayer Starter

As you are praying and meditating today, ask God to help you as you become more disciplined in the area of your health; which includes eating and exercising. Ask God to cover you as you start your journey towards a healthy lifestyle. Ask Him to help you to develop the right plan for your life that you might remain faithful to the regimen. Ask God to send the right people into your life in this season that will assist you as you begin your journey to **_BE!_** Healthy.

Scripture References

3 John 1:2 (New American Standard Version)

Study Notes:

BE! Healthy

Day Twelve

BE! Forgiving

Growing up as a little girl who was always doing something and getting in trouble my grandmother would say things to me like "Keep doing what you are doing, experience is the best teacher" or "Just live long enough and you'll understand what I'm saying"; or if I was really acting up she would tell my family "Don't tell her anything else she'll learn one day." Of course as a child I had no clue what she was talking about; but as I have had life experiences that have brought me great joy and incredible pain I now know the wisdom of her words. Life truly has been my best teacher. The lessons that life provides me and the way by which it provides them are unmatched by any other teaching tool. This may be because life's lessons are sometimes filled with unforgettable anguish that serves as a reminder to avoid the path that lead to the lesson at all costs. A good example of this for me is when I jumped into the deep end of a pool and I knew I could not swim. After my friend pulled me out of the water no one had to ever worry about me doing that again. I immediately learned the lesson. There was no need to repeat the same foolish act. Nope, I had it and I made a note to self as a reminder that read "I cannot swim."

However, life is always teaching; and there are lessons everywhere and in everything. One of the biggest and most difficult lessons life has taught me is the lesson that declares *BE!* Forgiving.

I am not speaking of forgiveness where the person that offended me asked for forgiveness; but rather having to forgive someone who has never and in some cases cannot ask for forgiveness. The heartache and disappointment that comes with this level of forgiveness I compare to scratching nails on a chalk board. It is painful to endure not because it affects me physically but because my soul cringes at the thought of not hearing the person admit that they were wrong or at the very least say they are sorry. To forgive someone who has never asked for it requires great humility and release of deep rooted and genuine feelings that may have been birthed as a result of neglect, abandonment, hurt, disappointment, unfaithfulness, misuse, being lied to or taken advantage of, and many other negative acts that occur as a result of being in relationship with other human beings. This lesson that proclaims to **_BE!_** Forgiving is one that I have faced on each new level of growth; and it is one that I admittedly have had varying degrees of success.

With this being said, as difficult as the mandate to **_BE!_** Forgiving may be it is necessary that we learn this lesson and grow to our next level in life. I use the word "grow" because there is simply no way to advance in anything when we are constantly dealing with the thing that is beneath us. Picture this if you will; see yourself standing on a ladder. You have one hand on the step in front of you with the intent to pull yourself up to the next step; but your other hand is holding on to the bush that has roots planted deep within the ground. As much as you would like to go higher up the ladder it will not happen until you let go of the bush. You will be stuck in the same position never going anywhere and never accomplishing anything. This is the lesson of forgiveness. While we are holding on to what someone else has done to us or in some case may still be doing we are harming ourselves alone. We will remain stuck between two decisions and our lives will continue to be stagnant until we let go and forgive.

Another example of being stuck is found in I Kings 18:21 when Elijah went before the people of Israel regarding their unwillingness or inability to make a decision. In the story, the people of Israel could not decide who they wanted to serve; God or Baal. Elijah said to them "How long will you waver between two opinions? If the Lord is God, follow Him, but if Baal is God, follow him. But, the people said nothing." (New International Version) God through the prophet was saying make a decision today. The time of going back and forth has ceased. God was saying to the children of Israel that it is time to choose Me or choose Baal; and I believe He is saying the same thing to us today. He is saying choose forgiveness and be set free or choose to hold on to unforgiveness and remain stuck on our current levels.

Further, there are many of us who are vacillating between holding on and letting go of unforgiveness. The very thought of forgiveness makes us angry but holding onto that anger has created a life for us that is producing very little joy and has made us extremely tired. This is a place that God does not want us to live. He is saying to us that we need to make the decision today to let go and move forward with our lives. It is time for us to **_BE!_** Forgiving. It is time to let go of the bush, the deeply rooted pain and the anxiety that it has brought into our lives. It is time for us to move on to the greatness that God has for us at the top of our ladders. It is time to let go of the hurt and the disappointments that are holding us captive in the things that happened to us many years ago. It is time to take back the power that we have given to that situation and place all of our efforts and energy into climbing our ladder and ascending to higher heights in our lives. Let us make the decision today to **_BE!_** Forgiving. Our next level is waiting for us.

Prayer Starter

As you are praying and meditating today, ask God to help you to let it go. Confess to him that you are angry and hurt. Tell him that you need Him to lead and guide you as you release the pain and disappointments of life and begin to climb your ladder towards success in Him. Speak to the "bush" that you have been holding onto and tell it that you do not need it any longer. Tell it that you are letting it go and giving it over to God. As you pray tell God that you trust Him to make your next level greater than the level you are own right now. Tell your past goodbye and grab ahold to your bright future that is ahead of you. It is time to **_BE!_** Forgiving.

Scripture Reference

I Kings 18:21 (New International Version)

BE! Forgiving

Day Thirteen

BE! Faithful

To have a friend that can be counted on at all times is priceless; and knowing there is someone that can be relied on in the time of need is immeasurable. As an entrepreneur and a person who has been in leadership positions throughout my life I have also discovered the necessity of having a team of people working with me that are just as committed to making the vision become reality as I am. This means that each team member who servers in an area of leadership must understand the overall mission of the project as well as the part they play in ensuring it is accomplished. In stretching this idea a bit further, I have grown to realize that not only should team members have a clear understanding of the project itself, but they should also spend a significant amount of time with the leader becoming familiar with the way in which she operates and knowledgeable about her approach to success. This is a key to life that many of us fail to grasp. It is not good enough to know and understand our jobs and the responsibilities associated with it; but we must also be clear about the expectations that our supervisors have in relation to us fulfilling our duties. It is important for us to know that while we are doing what we think measures up to a good job in the eyes of those we serve it may ultimately be viewed as something else entirely. This is why it is important for us to *BE!*

Faithful in doing what is expected of us and not what we have concluded is enough for us to do.

We see this exact scenario in Matthew 25:14-27. In these verses of scripture, we find a business owner. The owner is getting ready to take a trip, but before he does he calls three of his employees to a meeting. He gives one employee five talents, or money. He gives the other employee two talents; and the third employee receives one talent. Now, the bible says that each of them received their portion of talents based on their abilities alone. There were no other qualifications. The business owner knew each employee's ability to produce and again gave them each an assignment based only on that ability. As a result, after the owner left for his trip, the employee who received the five talents produced an additional five talents; and the employee with two talents produced an additional two talents. While on the other hand, the employee who was given one talent buried his talent in the ground and did not produce anything at all. When the owner returned from his trip the employees that produced the additional five and two talents received accolades. The owner said to them in verses 21 and 23 "Well done, good and faithful servant..." (King James Version)

Unfortunately for the employee who did not produce anything the response he received from the owner was completely different. In verses 25-27 the employee says:

> ... Lord, I knew you to be a hard man, reaping where you have not sown, and

gathering where you have not scattered seed. And I was afraid, and went and hid your talent in the ground. Look, there you have what is yours. But, his lord answered and said to him, you wicked and lazy servant, you knew that I reap where I have not sown, and gather where I have not scattered seed. So you ought to have deposited my money with the bankers, and at my coming I would have received my own with interest. (The Berean Study Bible)

In studying Matthew 25:21 and 23 we see that the employees who produced additional talents were called faithful or according to the Lexicon Study Bible they were deemed to be reliable. The owner was essentially saying to the two employees that he knew he could count on them to do exactly what he thought they would do in his absence which is to **_BE!_** Faithful and produce. This was not the case for the employee who buried his talent. This employee was called wicked and lazy; and at first read one may think that the owner's response was a bit harsh. But, in reading the next few verses it becomes clearer why the owner reacted the way he did. Note that the first two words the owner said to the employee after he called him wicked and lazy is "You knew…" We really do not have to read anything else after these two words. The fact that the employee had a working knowledge of who the owner was and what the owner expected is sufficient enough to understand the position that the owner took. The owner is saying to the employee that he did not have to guess at what the owner expected of him to do while he was gone. He said to the employee that even if he did not want to work hard at doubling the one talent, he should have at least put the talent in the bank and let interest accrue over time.

As a result, the frustration that the owner is expressing is understandable. The owner picked three specific employees to accomplish a goal by the time he returned. He trusted that each of them would ultimately produce because he gave them an assignment that was based on their individual abilities. Neither of them were set-up to fail. As a matter of fact each employee should have succeeded. When the employee with one talent went his own way and buried it in the ground his action showed that he was not reliable; he could not be trusted to **_BE!_** Faithful over the affairs of the owner. The owner expected the employee to produce not to bury the talent and then return it back to the owner in the manner in which it was given; and as this was the case for the employee, it is the same for us.

Many of us have buried our talents (gifts, abilities, callings) and we have done so for varying reasons, none of which would be sufficient enough excuse on that great day when we have to give our reports to the Lord. For others, if we have not buried our talents, we are certainly considering doing so. In addition, some of us have decided that doing something other than what God has said or going in another direction from what He has said is a better decision for our lives; and we are making this decision knowing that it is not a part of God's plan for us. We are consciously ignoring what we know and have experienced about God for the sake of not having to travel the world preaching the gospel, or singing in church, or working that secular job that we know we have been gifted to do. Further, others of us are doing a little bit of what God has said do, but we are not ready to fully commit to the call. In all of these varying degrees of being unproductive we must remember that we are running the risk of hearing God call us wicked and lazy servants. As you are meditating on this day remember that God expects us to **_BE!_** Faithful and productive to His plan for our lives as His plan must always take precedence over our own.

Prayer Starter

As you are praying and meditating today, ask God to give you the courage to dig up your buried talent. Ask Him to give you the confidence you need to step out on faith and work on your gift, talent or ability again. Tell Him that you want to be someone he can rely on to accomplish His will for your life. Ask God to show you how to be a producer in the area in which you have been called. Tell Him that you want to hear Him say to you "well done, good and faithful servant." Tell God that you will **_BE!_** Faithful.

Scripture References
Matthews 25:21 and 23 (King James Version)
Matthews 25:14-27 (The Berean Study Bible)

__BE!__ Faithful

_____
_____
_____
_____
_____
_____
_____
_____
_____
_____
_____
_____
_____
_____
_____
_____
_____
_____
_____
_____
_____
_____
_____
_____
_____
_____
_____
_____
_____
_____
_____
_____
_____
_____
_____

Day Fourteen

BE! Loving

I must confess that I am guilty. Before I even started to write the devotional for today, I had to be honest and say that this one was definitely for me! I stepped on my own toes as I wrote this devotional. You see I am that person who will give my last dollar to my family, to my friends and even to a stranger. I will give all of my time to ensure that someone's need is addressed. I am the person who has made everybody and everything a priority over my own need. I have the heart of a servant. I give to others with no expectation of ever getting anything in return. I will never let it be said that someone is in need of food and I have the ability to help them and I do not. I am the one that will go over and beyond the call of duty for anyone that I am in relationship with; but when it comes to putting that same effort into me I fall short time and time again. Yes, I am guilty of loving the world more than I love my own self; and of this I am sure.

With that being said, I know that I am not alone. Many of us are guilty of the exact same thing; but to live a healthy and balanced life we must adjust our approach. In Mark 12:28-31, Jesus was asked by one of the scribes which commandment is first out of all of the commandments. When Jesus replied, He not only addressed which one was first, but He also offered a second commandment to the scribe that He said was equal to the first. Jesus said in verse 31 that the second greatest commandment is that "… Thou shalt love thy neighbor as thyself…" (King James Version) Wait a minute. I know we have read this on many occasion, but let us take our time to really consider what this verse is saying. It says that we are supposed to love our neighbors in the same way that we LOVE OURSELVES. Wait, now what? Let us reverse it that we may see it in a different way. The verse is saying to us that in the SAME WAY that we love ourselves right now today let this be the SAME WAY that we love our neighbor. Wow!

Please take a moment to think about what Jesus is saying in Matthew 12:31. What is it revealing to you about you? Try not to rush pass this point because it is extremely important. Think about it long and hard. Would you want to transfer the love that you show to yourself on a daily basis to your neighbor? Many of us neglect our bodies by not sleeping or eating enough; but we would never refuse someone a place to sleep or food to eat. We speak negativity over our lives all day long. We tell ourselves we are fat, we are ugly, we are stupid, we are crazy; but we are the first to give other people compliments on their weight, their beauty or intelligence. We hold faults and mistakes against us never giving ourselves a chance to grow and mature into who God has ordained us to be; but we are the first to encourage others and remind them that God is forgiving and he is not holding their faults against them or even remembers their sin. We neglect ourselves and refuse to take time to go to the doctor to make sure that we are healthy; but we are the first ones at the hospital visiting the sick and shut-in. Many of us need a vacation like we need water. We have not taken time for us in years; but we are always on social media liking the pictures of our friends that were just on an Island for a week basking in the rays of the tropical sun, having the nerve to post on their pages "You deserve it, sis." I could go on and on, but I want to pose a question instead, why is it that we think it is alright for us to do more for others than we do for our own selves. Why do we not love us more?

I know. This is a hard one. God not only wants us to love ourselves totally and completely, but He needs us to do so. If we keep giving out more of ourselves than what we pour into ourselves we will eventually be empty and living on zero. Once we reach that point we will have nothing to give to anyone. There has to be a balance. We must get to a place where we see our own importance, our own value and our own worth. We cannot continue to be neglectful of our own need for the sake of fulfilling someone else's need. To continue to do so will eventually destroy us. It is imperative that you and me both reverse our course and get in line with the commandments of our God. We have to _**BE!**_ Loving to ourselves first and as we understand how to do so effectively, we can then love the world.

Prayer Starter

As you are praying and meditating today, ask God to show you how to _**BE!**_ Loving to you. Ask Him to help you to be comfortable with putting your needs first understanding that once you take care of you then you will be better equipped to take care of others. Ask Him to give you the strength to say no to those things that will attempt to pull you away from self-care and distract you from your goal of loving you first. Ask Him to give you wisdom as you make the right choices and adjustments for your life on your journey to *BE!* Loving to you.

Scripture Reference

Mark 12:28-31 (King James Version)

_BE!_ Loving

BE! Confident

How many times have you found yourself in a place where you felt unwanted or ineffective? Maybe your job sent you to a satellite office and when you arrived you were given the cold shoulder by the other employees. Maybe you were invited to minister at a church and in the middle of your ministry you could feel ice cycles fill the room; or maybe you were in a relationship with someone that no matter how hard you tried it seemed as if the love you were attempting to show was never received. Further, maybe your past behavior has cultivated a culture of mistrust that surrounds you everywhere you go. As a result, you are not given an opportunity to show that you are not the same person. Therefore, you are shut down before you even have a chance to prove your skill, ability, value or worth. To be in this position can be incredibly disheartening because one of the most difficult things to be is a changed person in the midst of people who remember you when. It takes a lot of strength and determination to *BE!* Confident in an environment where the sins from our past are continuously present in our lives.

I believe that this is the story of Onesimus in the book of Philemon. Onesimus was a runaway slave who had robbed Philemon some time prior to meeting Apostle Paul in Rome. Onesimus followed Paul and eventually became a believer in Jesus

Christ. At some point, Paul encourages Onesimus to return to Philemon; but when he sends him back, he advocates on his behalf. Paul tells Philemon in Philemon 11 "I beseech thee for my son Onesimus, who I have begotten in my bonds: which in time past was to thee unprofitable, but now profitable to thee and to me." King James Version) Paul says to Philemon, that he was coming to him on the behalf of Onesimus, who was now his son. I love this scripture because Paul was trying to create a window of opportunity for Onesimus to be seen for who he really was at his core; for who is has always been. You see the name Onesimus means useful, and a synonym for the word profitable is useful. As a result, Paul was saying to Philemon that not only could he vouch for Onesimus based on his affiliation with Paul; but if that was not sufficient enough, note that his very name exudes the character of which Paul speaks. He was saying that though Philemon concluded that Onesimus was not useful to him based on his acts; he was useful to them both in spite of his acts.

Moreover, one of the most beautiful parts about the Book of Philemon is the message that leaps off of the page that says our mistakes or bad acts cannot change our names. We are who God called us to be regardless to what anyone has to say about us. We may have done exactly what the world is saying we did; but, it does not change what God has spoken over our lives. Paul tells Philemon in his letter to him that he knows Onesimus has wronged him and for this he may be seen as unprofitable; but Paul declares that he is profitable. Paul is saying to Philemon to not allow your past experience with Onesimus to cloud your ability to see that he is exactly what his name declares and that is useful.

In the same respect, many of us are living the life of Onesimus right now. We have done some things in our lives that we are not proud of; but, we have accepted Jesus Christ into our lives and are now walking with Him. Unfortunately, the people who knew us prior to our conversion are still holding the past against us. I encourage you today to remember that just as Paul advocated for Onesimus with Philemon, you too have an advocate and His name is Jesus. Jesus is always speaking up for us. He is always fighting for us; and He will always remind us of who we are in Him. We have to **_BE!_** Confident in who and what God has called us to be in spite of our past missteps, wrong doings and failures. Our advocate died on the cross for our sins. He carried our sickness, diseases and sins with Him on the cross; and once we ask Him for forgiveness we can **_BE!_** Confident that our sins have been washed away to never be charged against us again.

Prayer Starter

As you are praying and meditating today, ask God to help you to **_BE!_** Confident in the face of opposition. Ask Him to remove any insecurity that may cause you to not move forward in the call over your life as a result of a past mistake or failure. Ask God to help you to close your ears to any negativity that is spoken over your life as you step out with confidence determined to do the work of the

Lord. Ask God to remind you of your name – victor, overcomer, entrepreneur, minister, educator, doctor, lawyer, and the like. Ask God to give you courage as you seek to **_BE!_** Confident in all that He has gifted and anointed you to be before the foundations of the world.

Scripture Reference

Philemon 11 (King James Version)

_BE!_ Confident

Day Sixteen

BE! Vigilant

This morning as I was meditating on the goodness of God I heard in my spirit the words "Don't come off of the wall. Your enemies will try to get you to come down; but don't come off of the wall." In a matter of seconds the next words I heard were *BE!* Vigilant. Both words seemed to be pressed deep within my spirit as I heard them over and over again. At some point I could see myself sitting at the top of a grey stone wall. As I sat on the wall I was also looking intently for what was coming next. I sat with anticipation of seeing who or what was going to attempt to convince me to leave my current position to be entertained; or more likely, to be distracted. As I sat I remained vigilant watching everything around me. I was very careful to observe everything and everyone that came into my path. Today God is telling us to continue to operate from the safety of the wall. It is from this place that we can see what our enemies are plotting against us and fend off all attacks before they even get started.

The scripture that I immediately thought of when God placed these words in my heart was Nehemiah 6:1-3. Here, Nehemiah encourages the people of Israel to rebuild the wall of Jerusalem. As with many things in life, a few people heard about what Nehemiah was doing and they attempted to sabotage the work. In verses 1-3, Nehemiah says:

When Sanballat, Tobiah, Geshem the Arab, and the rest of our enemies heard that I had rebuilt the wall and that there were no more breaks in it – even though I hadn't yet installed the gates – Sanballat and Geshem sent this message: "Come and meet with us at Kephrim in the valley of Ono." I knew they were scheming to hurt me so I sent messengers back with this: "I'm doing a great work; I can't come down. Why should the work come to a standstill just so I can come down to see you?" (The Message Bible)

The word that Nehemiah sent back is a very clear word of caution for us today. Nehemiah essentially asked his enemies "why should I stop what I am doing to entertain you?" My God! Family, please listen to and receive the wisdom of Nehemiah. We should not stop what we are building in life to shift our focus to what our enemies are saying about us. We should not leave the safety of the wall or project that we are working on to entertain anything that our enemies are trying to convince us to become a participant within. We must understand that the distractions will come more frequently once we start building because the enemy does not want us to complete the assignment that God has given to us. For this reason, we must **_BE!_** Vigilant. We must keep a careful watch for all dangers or difficulties that arise. We must remember that the work that we are involved in is a great work; and the enemy does not want us to complete the construction of our God-ordained structures.

As a result, the enemy is willing to do anything to keep us from completing our walls. This means that he will do actual physical harm to us if that is what it takes to stop us. Therefore, we must be discerning of who means us well and who does not. We must not allow everyone access into our lives because the work that we are accomplishing for God is a great. We must **_BE!_** Vigilant in all that we do and remain on the wall at all cost.

Prayer Starter

As you are praying and meditating today, ask God to help you to be **_BE!_** Vigilant. Ask Him to help you to be watchful at all times. Ask Him to help you to discern anyone that is in your life that seeks to hurt you. Ask God to help you to remain on the wall in the face of all conflict.

Scripture Reference

Nehemiah 6:1-3 (The Message Bible)

Study Notes:

BE! Vigilant

_____
_____
_____
_____
_____
_____
_____
_____
_____
_____
_____
_____
_____
_____
_____
_____
_____
_____
_____
_____
_____
_____
_____
_____
_____
_____
_____
_____
_____
_____
_____
_____

Day Seventeen

BE*!* Honest

As I was thinking about the devotional for today I started to wonder when it became the norm for us to tell lies as Christians. I tried to journey back in time in my mind to see if I could pinpoint the moment when telling the truth ceased to be popular. It appears as if it happened gradually over time. With each new twist in the delivery of the word of God and with each new varying perspective on the approach to self-care, we have abandoned the truth and have adopted a falsehood that is leading us down a road of denial and in some cases self-deception. The falsehood that I speak of is one that says we must not ever say how we are feeling if what we are experiencing is opposite of what the bible proclaims; or we must not ever talk about what we are fighting through spiritually whether it is sin or some other emotional battle because to do so represents a lack of faith and belief in God. Both of these ideas survive on the premise that we must go through our pains, sorrows and grief with a smile that lights up the world never revealing to anyone our heartache until we have made it on the other side of our situation in victory. Although this actually sounds great and there may be some element of truth to this perspective it is imperative that we ***BE!*** Honest with ourselves regarding our current condition insuring we do not fall into the trap of self-deception.

In my opinion, self-deception is the worst kind of deception because for Christians it mimics our faith-walk; and we must take care to discern between the two. Self-deception, though it may try to resemble faith is not faith at all. It is a practice that says although there is significant evidence to support a position that is different from the one that I have, I choose to deny the existence of that opposing position and diminish its relevance, significance or importance in my life. An example of this is when the doctor says to a patient that they have high blood pressure and need to cut back on their salt intake. Instead of accepting what the doctor says, the patient completely rejects the diagnosis deeming it to be untrue and continues on with her life as if it was never given. This is not faith. Faith does not deny the existence of a situation, but it instead meets that issue head on with the word of God that speaks directly to the problem. Faith says "Ok, I see you high blood pressure and I will no longer allow you to have residence in my life. I declare by the word of God that by the stripes of Jesus Christ I am healed and I will stand on God's word for my healing in this situation." Do you see the difference? One is a complete denial that something significant is taking place and the other is an acknowledgment of what is occurring along with the declaration of what the word of God has to say concerning its existence. As Christians, we want to ***BE!*** Honest about the things that are going on in our lives. We do not want to ignore a diagnosis from our doctors thinking that in doing so we are operating in faith. This is not the case. To ignore is to open a gateway for self-deception to rule in our lives.

In the same vein, we also do not want to deceive ourselves when it relates to sin in our lives. The bible is clear when it says in Romans 3:23 "for all have sinned, and come short of the glory of God." (New King James Version) None of us are perfect. We all make mistakes. Therefore, walking around as if we have it all together and have never let God down a day in our spiritual lives is an unnecessary and futile act because God knows better. In I John 1:8, the bible addresses the idea of self-deception and its relation to sin. The verse says "If we say that we have no sin, we deceive ourselves, and the truth is not in us." (King James Version) Unless your name is Jesus Christ the son of the living God, there is not one person that has walked this earth that has not, is not or will not sin. It is a part of our growth process as followers of Christ. We are not perfect, we make mistakes; and that is alright by God.

As a result, I encourage you to find someone that you trust to keep what you share with them in confidence and let them know what is going on with you. If you are in pain emotionally, dealing with a sickness, fighting through a recurring issue relating to sin in your life, find someone and talk through your situation. Please know that ignoring it is not the way to handle the problem. We must meet our issues head on and face-to-face. Forget what you may have heard someone say in the Christian faith about not talking about your faults and short comings. Express your failures to someone. Release the idea of carrying your hurt and disappointments alone until your situation gets better. You do not have to walk around as a person with dual personalities being one person to the world around you; and another on the inside. ***BE!*** Honest with yourself, with others and with God. Declare that in your life self-deception ends today!

Prayer Starter

As you are praying and meditating today, ask God to help you to ***BE!*** Honest. Ask Him to help you to stop the self-deception. Ask God to show you how to walk in faith trusting that though the situation may be contrary to His word He is able to heal, deliver and set us free. Ask Him to lead you to the person that will hear your truth, hold it in confidence and pray with you until you receive the victory over sickness, depression, family issues, financial issues, emotional issues, or whatever you have been ignoring or denying the existence thereof.

Scripture References

Romans 3:23 (New King James Version)
I John 1:8 (King James Version)

_**BE!**_ Honest

Day Eighteen

BE! Gracious

A few years ago I met a friend for lunch. As we were sitting in the restaurant eating I glanced up at the same time that the waitress was approaching our table with a tray filled with glasses of ice cold water. It appeared that as soon as I made eye contact with her she began to stumble. The glasses on the tray immediately started to rock back and forth; and before anyone could do anything to stop the inevitable, cold glasses of ice water toppled over the tray and landed on me. Needless to say, my clothes, my face and seemingly my entire body was drenched in water. The waitress was mortified by her actions. She apologized profusely and ran to get as many napkins as she could find to help dry me off. The manager came to our table and he too apologized to me over and over again. The manager paid for our lunch and told me to bring him my dry cleaning bill. The whole time everyone was attending to me my friend had a look of shear surprise and amazement on his face and not for the reasons one would think. His look of surprise and amazement was not because of the incident with the water, but my reaction to it. Though I was drenched in ice cold water from my head to my torso my response to the incident amazed him. Not one time did I raise my voice neither did I complain. I did not tell the young lady that she was clumsy and that she needed to learn how to walk and carry a tray at the same time. I did not tell the manager that he was doing a poor job with training his staff. As a matter of fact, I did not get upset with them at all. In that moment, I had a choice. I could have made a bad situation worse by yelling at the waitress and berated her. I could have yelled at the manager and given him a stern look of disapproval; but I chose another route. I immediately decided that tensions were high enough and that I did not want to add to an already stressful situation. I did not want to contribute to the feeling of shame and embarrassment that the waitress was already experiencing. Therefore, I chose to be kind-hearted and compassionate. I chose to **_BE!_** Gracious.

It was evident that the waitress had made a mistake. There was no intent to do me harm. She simply stumbled and the glasses she was carrying toppled over. I could not image me giving any other response to that situation; but, in most cases, this is not the same scenario between us and God. Many times, we have acted with intent and have gone in the opposite direction of the word of God. We often choose people, things and situations that we know are not the best for us; and we act in ways that are offensive to our Christian faith. Yet God is still kind and compassionate towards us. With all of our bad decisions and our wrong actions our God is still gracious to us. As a matter of fact the bible says in Ephesians 2:8 that "For by grace are we saved through faith; and that not of yourselves: it is the gift of God..." (King James Version) Here, the verse is saying that it is because of God's grace alone that we are saved and not our works. It is because He chose to show us kindness that we are even in relationship with Him today. It is because He decided to gift us with grace that we have an opportunity to get our lives together every day, and grow into being a better us.

For this reason, we must strive to live a life where we are extending grace to those around us. We are all human and there may be times where someone will stumble and offend us with their actions. When this happens, it is not the time to berate the person with our quick wit or humiliate them because of their error. Our responsibility is to be kind and show them compassion. This will be easy for us to accomplish as long as we remain humble and remember that God extends grace to us every single day for things that we intentionally do that offends Him and the gospel that we believe. If God can do that for us we can choose to **_BE!_** Gracious to others as well.

Prayer Starter

As you are praying and meditating today, ask God to help you to **_BE!_** Gracious. Ask Him to show you how to be kind to those who have offended you. Ask God to help you identify people that you need to extend grace to even though they may have intentionally offended you. Ask God to help you to be compassionate to others as He is towards you every day.

Scripture Reference

Ephesians 2:8 (King James Version)

_BE!_ Gracious

Day Nineteen

BE! Fearless

It seems like every five years or somewhere in this timeframe that God challenges me to expand and do something that I have never imagined doing. It is truly amazing how it happens. For example, when God put it in my heart to go to law school the thought of it really blew my mind because I could not reconcile it with all of the other things I had going on in my life. I struggled for a long time to understand the who, what and the how of this mandate. To be perfectly honest, the idea of it made me really nervous. As a result, I procrastinated for a very long time. I bought the books to start studying for the LSAT (the law school entrance test); and as soon as I would sit down to begin to study I would allow myself to become distracted. Another example of God challenging me to stretch into uncharted areas is writing this devotional. Though I have considered writing books in the past, I never thought about writing a devotional. I was actually on board to write. I have thought about the kind of books I would write over the years, but I never fathomed writing a devotional. When God said write and then He said devotional, I did not understand the magnitude of the request until I started typing the first words. If I am honest, the requirement to be as open as I have to be to accomplish what God wants me to accomplish is extremely scary. Opening up my life in this way is taking a level of boldness and confidence in God that I did not know I had or even needed; and making sure that I am "rightly dividing" the bible adds another level of uncertainty in my ability to accomplish this goal as well. God is constantly tugging on my heart to launch out into the deep and reinvent or add on to the building that He calls Teta. He is continuously calling me to new experiences; and with each new call I battle with fear that manifests in varying ways such as procrastination. At this point in my life though, I have spent enough time with God to know that when He is leading me to do something that His plan is perfect and it will manifest. The key here is that I must find the strength to **_BE!_** Fearless in my pursuit of God's plan for my life. When I do, I will see Him do marvelous works on my behalf and for His people; and the same goes for you as well.

The bible says in 2 Timothy 1:7 that "God has not given us the spirit of fear, but of power and of love and of a sound mind." (New King James Version) The word fear here is translated to mean timidity and timidity means to lack courage or confidence. As a result the scripture is saying that God has not given us a spirit that lacks courage or confidence, but He has given us the opposite of them both. The scripture says that He has given us power and not only that, but He has also given us a sound mind. Now, the words "sound mind" are translated to mean self-discipline. Therefore, the verse is not only reminding us that we are a powerful people in God; but it is also saying that we are a people of self-discipline as well. Let us recap. The verse in 2 Timothy is really saying that we are a "powerful people who are courageous, confident and self-disciplined." Wow! I really love the bible. This verse of scripture is proclaiming to us that we should **_BE!_** Fearless because our entire being opposes the idea of us living any other way. Our entire being runs against the thoughts or the ideologies that fear seeks to impart within us. We are not a fearful people. At our core, we are powerful, courageous, confident and self-disciplined; and when we enter a room everything about us states this exact fact. We are fearless.

If we are able to grab a good hold to this concept, we will begin to see our lives change drastically. All we have to do is walk in the confidence that already lies within us. There is no need to worry. We can trust that if God said that we are going to complete a work that it will happen. The only requirements for us are that we step into what He said without hesitation; and that we exercise self-discipline in the process. We must begin to move out on His word. We can no longer allow distractions to enter into our lives and divert our attention from what we should be doing for God and ultimately for ourselves. This means that we may have to turn the television off, only talk to our families and friends at specified times during the day until our dreams have manifested, or stop spending money eating out every day and begin to save for the vision. Whatever is needed for us to fulfill the mandate on our lives, we must do it; and exercising self-disciple is required.

Let us **_BE!_** Fearless today and do something that we know God has been leading us to do, but we have not stepped into it because we have allowed fear to rule over our lives. Today, allow courage and confidence to reign supreme. Let us walk into what God has ordained for our lives without hesitation, delay or distraction.

Prayer Starter

As you are praying and meditating today, ask God to help you to **_BE!_** Fearless. Ask Him to show you what He has ordained for you to do; and then ask Him to help you to walk in the courage and confidence that is already within you. Ask God to help you schedule your life better, to make a plan that you walk in self-discipline not allowing yourself to become distracted from the call of God for your life.

Scripture Reference

2 Timothy 1:7 (New King James Version)

Study Notes:

_BE!_ Fearless

Day Twenty

BE! Transformed

In thinking about the devotional for today for some reason the very first picture I saw in my mind was an image of the cartoon and now movie *The Transformers*. Are you familiar with that movie? It is the one where the robots are able to transform themselves into cars, planes, birds and other such things. I remember watching the cartoon when I was younger. It was actually one of my favorite cartoons and I could not wait for it to come on television. I loved everything about this this cartoon. One of my favorite parts about it was the theme song. When it was time for the show to begin, I would rush in front of the television and stand there waiting for the theme song to start. From the very first note that was played I would start singing at the top of my lunges "Transformers, more than meets the eye, Transformers, robots in disguise." I would sing it over and over again as loud as I could; but as a child I could not see or understand the significance of the theme song as I do today. You see as people, not only as Christians, we must begin to recognize that we too are transformers because there is more to us than what other people can see. For many of us, our outer shell is covering up the power that lies within us. In the cartoon, the robots could do things in their transformed state that they could not do otherwise. For example, the robots could use weapons that were not available to them in their other form and they appeared to be stronger and could move faster as well. In their transformed state the robots gained power to fight in the battle that could not be accessed otherwise; and, as it was for the robots so it is for us. There is strength and power lying within us that we have not tapped into. There is more to us than what people and in some cases we even know. It is time for us to discover our hidden power. It is time for us to *BE!* Transformed.

In Romans 12:2 the bible says "Do not conform to the pattern of this world, but be transformed by the renewing of your mind." (New International Version) According to Webster's dictionary, the word transformed means to make a thorough or dramatic change in form, appearance or character of, to change in character or condition. In addition, the word change means to be converted; and converted means to become obsolete. Lastly, the word renewing means to make new spiritually, to regenerate, to make extensive changes in or to rebuild. As we dissect the words in Romans 12:2 we discover that though the transformers in the cartoon and subsequently the movie changed back and forth from one form to another throughout the show; this is not God's plan for our lives. Here, the scripture is telling us that the ultimate goal for our lives is for our character to be changed in such a way that it becomes obsolete when it is transformed into something new. God does not want us to vacillate between the old and the new. He wants us to *BE!* Transformed into our better selves; and the way for us to accomplish this goal is by taking an active role in changing the way that we think. God wants our thought processes to be spiritually regenerated or restored to a higher state that we may ultimately understand what His perfect will is for our lives and then operate in this state accordingly.

Moreover, Apostle Paul, the author of Romans 12:2, is encouraging us to not allow ourselves to get caught up in the ways in which other people or systems of our world approach life in character or in thinking. He is saying that there is another way for us to view our present conditions whether individual or societal; but the only way for us to see, know or even understand this way is for us to **_BE!_** Transformed in our thinking. Now, the question to be answered is how do we become transformed in our thinking? How is it accomplished? We have to remember as stated in Isaiah 55:8-9 that God's ways or not our ways and His thoughts are not our thoughts; and that the two thought processes and approaches to life are as vastly different as the heavens are separated from the earth. As a result, in order for us to comprehend God's will and plan, we must restore and refresh our minds with the words of the Bible every day. As we spend time studying the word, praying and meditating we will begin to discover that the way we used to process problems, struggles and issues will have become different. As we study and begin to apply the scriptures in the bible to everyday situations, we will realize that we are becoming stronger and more self-assured of our perspective on life. The more time we spend with God in prayer we will start to recognize a change within us. We will notice that we are viewing the world and its systems no longer from our vantage point alone, but also from God's perspective through the verses of scripture in the bible.

Further, there is purpose for transformation and it is that we understand God's plan. We will never understand the ways of God or even His will until we are converted into a new being whose thinking has been restored. We must spend time with God by studying His word, praying and meditating. When we do these things we will begin to see a difference in how we approach and perceive our lives and things around us. In order for us to **_BE!_** Transformed we will have to put in some work; but we can be assured that with transformation comes a power that we have not tapped into ever before in our lives.

Prayer Starter

As you are praying and meditating today, ask God to help you to **_BE!_** Transformed. Ask Him to show you how to study the bible and seek Him in prayer that you may be able to understand His thoughts and His ways more clearly. Ask God to help you to understand His plan that you may know His good and acceptable, and perfect will for your life. Ask God to reveal to you the power that lies within you as you walk in your transformed state.

Scripture References

Romans 12:2 (New International Version)
Isaiah 55:8-9

Study Notes:

BE! Transformed

Day Twenty-One

BE! Enough

Many times we find ourselves on the treadmill of life pushing to be some person that momma and daddy, friends, family or some other person says we should be. For example, someone may haven spoken a word or positive affirmation over our lives in the past and because it sounded good we ran with it expecting that if we worked hard enough we would see their words manifest. In addition, some of us may have been "born into" what we were going to do in life. For instance, maybe your parents are doctors and the expectation all of your life has been that you would be a doctor as well. Therefore, you have spent years in school and hundreds of thousands of dollars to fit into the mold that was prepared for you by those who mean you well and love you immensely. In addition, maybe you do not fall into either of the aforementioned categories where you have been directed to a path. As a result, you may be going through life flapping your wings but never taking off and flying. You have tried any and every new opportunity that has been offered seemingly grasping for straws in an attempt to find your way through life. Though each of these paths to obtaining success is completely different they all carry a poisonous trait that if left unchecked could have us pursuing a career, ministry, education or some other life goal for the wrong reasons.

You see there are times when we may be pushing ourselves to accomplish something not because we believe it is exactly what we have always wanted to do or who we envisioned ourselves being; but it is because we feel like we have something to prove to the people in our circles. If left unaddressed, the desire to prove to people that they were right or in some cases wrong, may drive us to a place of complete misery and possible self-destruction. One of my favorite quotes from the illustrious author and poet Maya Angelou is "You alone are enough. You have nothing to prove to anybody." This is a truth that we have to live within every day. We, the way that we are right now at our core is enough. Whether we become a doctor, lawyer, singer, actor, teacher, coach, minister, author or not, we must remind ourselves that in our current state WE ARE ENOUGH. We have absolutely nothing to prove to anyone. The key to our success is within us and it is not attached to us producing proof to the people who love or in some instances dislike us. We have to remember that to **_BE!_** Enough requires no effort at all. We just are.

In 2 Peter 1:3 the bible says "His divine power has given us everything required for life and godliness through the knowledge of him who called us by his own glory and goodness." (Christian Standard Bible) The author is saying that God has given us exactly what we need to be successful in this life. What is required has already been provided to us. We only need to take the time to discover through prayer and meditation what provisions have been made and how we need to implement what has been provided in our

156

lives. God did not consult any other person, not even us, when He gave us what we needed for life. As a result, we should not find it to be wrong or disrespectful if we chose to not consult others on what God has designed us to be. To **_BE!_** Enough is an act of our wills alone because we already have within us all that we need; we just have to walk it out until it manifests.

Further, spending time trying to prove to others that we are walking out our lives the way it was meant to be lived is an unnecessary and futile act. Most people will not understand God's plan for us and that is perfectly alright. They do not have to, but we do. It is our jobs to know what God is saying and go after it with all of our hearts. Our families may not understand our choices, friends may be concerned because what we are doing does not resemble anything that may have been discussed with them in prior conversation; but we cannot allow anyone else's perspective on our lives to distract us from accomplishing what we are on this earth to fulfill.

Therefore, today, take a moment to consider your life. Is what you are doing exactly what you want to do or are you doing it because it is what others have said you should do? Is it what you have seen yourself doing all of your life? Is it something that brings you joy and happiness? Is what you are pursuing right now something that you have been called to do or is it something that other people are successful at doing and you think you can be successful at it as well? Please take a moment today and consider your life. Remember that there are no outside forces that can interrupt God's divine plan for you. The only person that can do so is you. Do not allow the desire to prove that someone else is wrong and you right cause you to continue down a road that was never yours to travel. You have nothing to prove. To **_BE!_** Enough only requires that you operate from the perspective that God has given you all that you need for life. You only have to walk in that understanding; no proof needed.

Prayer Starter

As you are praying and meditating today, ask God to give you revelation on what it means for you to **_BE!_** Enough. Ask Him to show you if what you are doing right now as a career or ministry or some other work is His plan for your life or someone else's. Ask God to help you to see what you should be pursuing and how it lines up with what He has given you for your life. Ask God to give you understanding as you make the necessary adjustments to walk in and who you already are without feeling like you have to prove to others that what you are doing is right and their perspectives are wrong. Ask God to cover you with His arms of protection as you make some hard turns to readjust yourself to walk on the road of success that He designed for your life and not the one designed by others.

Scripture Reference

2 Peter 1:3 (Christian Standard Bible)

Study Notes:

BE! Enough

Day Twenty-Two

BE! Wealthy

What came across your mind when you read the devotional topic for today? Did you immediately equate the idea of wealth with money? Were you able to expand the concept of wealth into other areas of life other than currency? If not, do not be discouraged. Many people when considering the idea of wealth are only able to associate it with riches; but it expands beyond this perspective. As a matter of fact, according to Vocabulary.com the word wealth is derived from the old English word wela which means to have "happiness and prosperity in abundance." I am convinced that as human beings it is not our desire to have "wela" in our finances only, but to also have it in every area of our lives. Therefore, as we discuss what it means to *BE!* Wealthy, I am encouraging each of us to examine our lives as a whole. I do not want us to focus on what we have or do not have monetarily only; but let us take an honest inspection of our lives in its entirety.

To *BE!* Wealthy is a concept that in some respect has been watered down to the point that some may believe that it is unattainable; but I argue that all of us are living a wealthy life to a degree. As a result all of us have something of value to offer the world. According to Oxford dictionary, the word wealth is defined as having a large amount of money, property, or valuable possessions. The adjective for the word wealth is wealthy and it

162

means to have a great deal of money, resources or assets. For our purposes here, let us focus on the words valuable possessions and resources. Ask yourself, what valuable possessions or resources do you have whereby others consider you to be wealthy. What knowledge do you possess or what skills do you have to offer that people specifically seek you out for advice or assistance? Really stop and think about these questions. There is wealth already inside of each of us. We only have to discover what it is and operate accordingly. Once we understand the width and breath of this wealth we can then make the necessary adjustments to obtain the riches that we may desire.

Deuteronomy 8:18 is a perfect scripture for us to study in relation to our devotional. The verse says "But remember the Lord your God, for it is he who gives you the ability to produce wealth..." (New International Version) In Deuteronomy chapter 8, the children of Israel are being prepared to enter into the promise land. Prior to entering they are admonished to not forget the times of humility and struggle they endured in the wilderness when they reach the promise land. Moreover, not only are they are reminded of the difficulties that they faced in the wilderness, but they are also reminded about the provisions that were afforded them as well. In this verse of scripture, they are presented with all of the goodness that the promise land has to offer while at the same time being encouraged to never forget the journey they made to get there. As they are preparing for entrance into the promise land the author in verse 18 says to the children of Israel to remember that the ability to obtain wealth was not derived from them, but it came from the Lord. In other words, God is the one that gave them what they needed to get wealth.

Further, as we examine Deuteronomy 18:8 a little closer, let us not read it too fast as we may miss the beauty that lies within the verse. As previously stated, the scripture says that the Lord is the one who gives us the ability to **_BE!_** Wealthy. He is the originator of our wealth plans and He has placed within us the ideas, skills and abilities necessary for us to be highly valued within our sphere of influence. He is the one that makes us a resource for the people in our circles that the knowledge we have to offer is deemed beneficial. Therefore, the question that must be asked today is what kind of wealth lies within you? What resources has the Lord given to you that attract people to you? If you are able to discover the answers to these questions you will then be able to access the riches that your heart desires.

It is important for us to note that we are already wealthy in some area of life; and it is in that area that we need to focus. For example, I love people and I seek to be a light and a beacon of positivity wherever I go. This characteristic is a place of wealth for me; and this aspect of my life draws people to me thereby creating an opportunity for me to be a resource to others. As we discover the abundance of resources, possessions, knowledge or skills that lie within us we can then understand how our lives affect the people we are in relationship with on a daily basis. We may also discover opportunity to **_BE!_** Wealthy from the perspective of riches as a result.

Prayer Starter

As you are praying and meditating today, ask God to teach you how to **_BE!_** Wealthy in every area of your life. Ask Him to show you the wealthy place that lies within you. Ask Him to reveal to you how you affect the people in your circle and how you are a resource to those that are in your sphere of influence. Ask God to show you how to not only be a resource, but to also **_BE!_** Wealthy from a financial perspective as well.

Scripture Reference

Deuteronomy 8:18 (New International Version)

_BE!_ Wealthy

Day Twenty-Three

BE! Kind

I read a post not too long ago on Facebook where the person asked a question that I answered fairly quickly. The question was "Is it alright for us to be angry with God?" I responded "Yes, He can handle it!" When I consider the question as well as my response my heart is filled with a tremendous amount of gratefulness because we truly do serve a God who understands all aspects of our character and design. Our God is not intimidated by us nor is He scared off by our outbursts of anger or temper tantrums that we sometimes have because we do not like the direction in which our lives are going. God is patient with us and He loves us in and through all of our mess ups; and He never turns His back on us because we falter. He cares for us; and more than that, He loves us completely. This is so awesome! Our God is the greatest example of what kindness looks like and how it should be expressed toward others. Therefore, God's response to us should serve as a guide to how we respond to others as well. Although, unfortunately, as followers of Christ, we do not always capture God's spirit and our reaction to each other sometimes lacks love and compassion. As a result, we may appear to be carrying anger and bitterness within us that may ultimately hinder our relationships and the free flow of blessings into our lives. For this reason, we must make every effort to *BE!* Kind to those we love and to those that have shown us evil as well to give the Christ that we serve an opportunity to be seen in us and through us.

In Luke 6:35, the bible says "But love your enemies, and do good, and lend, expecting nothing in return; and your reward will be great, and you will be sons of the Most High; for He Himself is kind to ungrateful and evil men." (New American Standard Bible) Here, according to the Lexicon Study Bible, the word "kind" is translated to mean serviceable or good. This verse of scripture is saying to us that we must be in service and we must do good to those that are ungrateful and evil. Wow! Now, I know this is not an easy task. I have had to deal with ungrateful and evil people in my life and the thought of helping them or being good to them was quite overwhelming. I understand how you may be feeling. None of us want to be taken advantage of; and we all want to be appreciated for what we do for others. What we have to glean from this verse of scripture is not that God wants us to be a door map for people; but rather that He wants us to remain in a position to receive the reward that comes from us being in service and good to our enemies. The key here is that we not block the flow of blessings coming into us because we have closed our hand of giving to others, including our enemies. We must **_BE!_** Kind to everyone.

Moreover, take a moment to consider the people in your life that may be in need and you have closed your hand of service and goodness towards them forever? Now, just for a moment think about the offenses that you have made in your relationship with God. Is God justified in turning the faucet of blessings over your life off because of these offenses? If He does turn the blessings off where would you be right now or in the future? It is a scary thought to have to live life without the hand of God maneuvering people, places and things in our lives! It is for this reason that God does not want us to stop showing kindness to those that have offended us. We need each other and most people do not realize that until they are completely down and out and there is no one around to provide them with assistance. To be in a position to show the love and kindness of God to someone in need, especially someone that showed you evil is a beautiful example of God in operation here on the earth.

Prayer Starter

As you are praying and meditating today, ask God to show you how to **_BE!_** Kind. Ask Him to reveal to you the people that you have cutoff who are in need of your service. Ask God to heal your heart and strengthen you as you seek to do good to your enemies and not evil. Ask Him to help you to be more like Him as you open your hand of kindness allowing your reward to freely flow into your life.

Scripture Reference

Luke 6:35 (New American Standard Bible)

_**BE!**_ Kind

Day Twenty-Four

BE! Encouraged

There are times in our lives when it appears that we cannot shake off of us feelings that are contrary to the word of God and the life that we proclaim to live as Christians. The feelings of depression, fear, discouragement, loneliness, inadequacy, low self-esteem, and more will at times attempt to ensnare us and become rooted within our spirits. We must be mindful of this because if we are not we may find ourselves heeding the call of these feelings and submitting to them as well. In our devotional for today, I want us to be honest about this truth. More likely than not, there is no one with you as you are reading this devotional. As a result, you do not have to pretend like there is nothing bothering you. In this moment, you do not have to act as if you feel strong when the truth is you do not. In recent months, I have heard of dozens of Christians ending their lives because they were dealing with an overwhelming amount of depression and for whatever reason they could not work through the issues that were causing them to feel this pain. Yes, I use the word pain because I have dealt with depression in my life and at the root of it was pain; and at the center of it was pain. Whether it was pain from the death of a loved one, the loss of a job, the ending of a marriage, or the repossession of material things that I had worked really hard to obtain, at the root of my feelings of depression was pain that was left unaddressed. I will not pretend that the devotional for today will fix everything that is ailing you; but what I want you to know is that you are not alone. We are all, and we have all, and we all will be faced with feelings that do not always represent the joy of the Lord. It is in these times that we have to know that we are not by ourselves; and though it may take time and effort on our parts, we can ultimately **_BE!_** Encouraged again.

In 1 Samuel 30:6 the bible says "And David was greatly distressed; for the people spoke of stoning him, because the soul of all of the people was grieved, every man for his sons and for his daughters: but David encouraged himself in the Lord his God." (American King James Version) Here, David and the men that fought with him in battle returned to their home and discovered that their families and other possessions had been taken captive by their enemies. All of the men, including David, experienced a great loss; but instead of the men rallying around David, they discussed killing him. In that moment, David was not only faced with the loss of his family, but he was also faced with the potential loss of his life by those that he fought with in battle. This is an awful place for David to be in because he was left with no one to support him. David had no one to lean on in the midst of great trial, heartache and stress. The people that he thought he could count on were plotting how they were going to kill him. Therefore, the scripture says that in the midst of one of the most difficult moments in David's life, he "encouraged himself in the Lord his God." In this verse, the word "encouraged" is translated to mean strengthened. Now, the bible does not say how long it took David to get to the place where he began to strengthen himself in the Lord; but the time frame is not what is relevant. The most important point to me here is that in the middle of his brokenness David knew exactly where to go and that was to the Lord his God. It was in the Lord that David found the strength that he needed to take back what his enemies had stolen from him; and it is in the Lord's presence that we can find strength to take back our joy and overcome the feelings that are contrary to the word of God as well.

Further, in Psalm 16:11, which was written by David, the scripture says "… in thy presence is fullness of joy; at thy right hand *there are* pleasures for evermore." (King James Version) This is one of my most favorite scriptures because it reminds us that everything that we have need of we can find it in the Lord. If we lack peace, hope, support from others, wisdom, guidance, understanding or any other thing we can find what we need in God. This is such an awesome word to receive because it helps us to know that we are not alone in our efforts to be what is required of us to be. We only have to enter into the presence of the Lord to find the strength that we need. I can only image David worshiping his way into God's presence as this is what he was known throughout scripture to do. As you may be dealing with issues that have left you feeling sad, depressed or alone remember that there is strength in God's presence. Therefore, I say to you today to ___BE!___ Encouraged not in your strength alone, but rather in the strength of our Lord.

Prayer Starter

As you are praying and meditating today, ask God to help you to enter into His presence and be strengthened by Him. Tell Him about the feelings that you are dealing with; and ask Him to show you how to overcome those feelings through worship. As you spend time in God's presence, ask God to lead you to people that will support you as you work out what you are feeling. Ask Him to give you daily reminders that you are not by yourself and that there are other people waiting to support and love you right where you are today. Ask God to help you to **_BE!_** Encouraged in Him.

Scripture References

I Samuel 30:6 (American King James Version)
Psalm 16:11 (King James Version)

_**BE!**_ Encouraged

Day Twenty-Five

BE! Free

Have you ever thought about what it truly means to *BE!* Free? Have you ever taken a "freedom inspection" of your life to determine if you are living a bondage free existence? If you have not I would like for you to stop reading right now and take some time to ponder these questions. Do not go any further until you have considered the idea of being free and how it is applicable to your life. Think about every area of your life including your family, spiritual life, friends, and employment, as well as your physical and mental health; make a list. Then ask yourself are you totally and completely free in every area of your life. Be honest with yourself. Are there any areas where you are bond by people and their opinions? Are you the person that everyone in the family counts on for support? Has this position in the family become a weight that now has you mentally and emotionally bond because you do not know how to say no? Are you a member of a church that has so many rules and regulations to follow that you are now more bond in your Christian walk than you were before salvation? Think about every aspect of your life and pick up reading in the next paragraph when you are done.

Now that you have taken the time to consider the areas in your life where you are bond let us examine what it means to *BE!* Free from these bondages. The bible says in John 8:36 "So, if the

Son makes you free, you will be free indeed." (New American Standard Version) The phrase "makes you free" literally means to be exempt from liability. It also means that we are not slaves or under restraint any longer. As a result, the verse is saying that when Jesus makes us free we have no further liability to the thing that has been holding us captive. John 8:36 is proclaiming that we do not owe anyone anything at all. Here, the verse is saying that we can operate in this life knowing that we are free in Christ because nothing can affect or infect the liberties provided to us through Jesus. This means that when we accept Jesus into our lives as Lord and Savior, we also receive liberty and freedom from all bondages that were holding us before salvation as well as all bondages that would seek to hold us afterwards. For these reasons, we must begin to apply the word of God to our lives in such a way that we resist anything and any person that attempts to stifle the freedom and liberty given to us through Christ Jesus.

In addition, we must **_BE!_** Free to work the plan of God for our lives without hindrances from others. I believe that each of our goals is to be the people that we have been designed to be before we were conceived in our mother's womb. Unfortunately, there are times when religious systems may attempt to control our efforts to be that person, thereby serving as a mechanism that keeps us from accomplishing our goals. This is the perspective from which Paul was speaking when he wrote John 8:36. Paul was saying to the churches of Galatia that he did not want them to operate by the law, but by faith. He reminded them that the law had no place in their lives and that they should interact with each other by faith and in love alone.

Further, it is important for us to understand and believe that John 8:36 is applicable to all areas of our lives not only our Christian experiences. It is God's plan that we live a life of freedom and liberty not a life of bondage. It does not matter if we are talking about freedom in our marriages, friendships, careers, nutrition or even our Christian beliefs, we must not allow ourselves to live a life of bondage to anyone or anything. To do so does not represent the will of God for our lives.

Moreover, if we are concerned about what other people think or how they feel about us making certain steps in our lives we are not operating in freedom. Let us consider again the areas where you have identified that you are in bondage. What type of bondage are you under? Is it in relation to people because you have a hard time saying no? Are you in bondage to credit cards or other financial debt? Are you in bondage because you do not eat enough or maybe you eat too much? Are you in bondage to the opinions of others? Are you unable to make any decisions on your own without the backing of other people? I encourage you to spend some quality time considering the devotional for today. Make every effort to pull yourself out of and away from what has been holding you captive because it is time for you to **_BE!_** Free. It is time for you to live a life of liberty.

Prayer Starter

As you are praying and meditating today, ask God to show you the areas of your life where you have been living a life of bondage. As you identify each area ask Him to give you strength to overcome those places of bondage and rise above what has been holding you captive. Ask God to help you to see your value and your worth that you will be able to say no to those things that seek to control you. Ask Him to help you to be bold in your pursuit of life not waiting for others to confirm you before you launch out into something new. Ask God for His help as you seek to **_BE!_** Free in Him.

Scripture Reference

John 8:36 (New American Standard Version)

Study Notes:

BE! Free

Day Twenty-Six

BE! Focused

As I am typing the devotional for today I feel like I want to say to you to turn and tell your neighbor to *BE!* Focused. I do not know if someone is around you or not; but, just find somebody and tell them to *BE!* Focused. If you are by yourself, go stand in front of a mirror and tell yourself to *BE!* Focused. Life is too short for us to continue allowing time to pass us by. It is time for us to set a plan of action and move forward towards accomplishing our goals. Now is the season for us to begin living the life that we have been dreaming about for years. It is time to *BE!* Focused on starting our careers, reclaiming our health, growing spiritually, spending more time with our families, obtaining our education or traveling the world. We have to accept the reality that time is not waiting on us to make moves. One of the most shocking things to see is a picture of a family member or friend celebrating the birth of their baby on Facebook and then seemingly at the blink of an eye another picture scrolls down the timeline and that same baby is graduating from high school. Have you had this experience? Instances like this have been the greatest motivators for me to stop procrastinating and start making significant moves in my life. God has not called us to live vicariously through our family and friends on social media; but He has given to each of us destiny and purpose that we must fulfill. One of the main ingredients for accomplishing God's plan is focus.

We cannot allow distractions to come into our lives and hinder us from reaching our goals. We must **_BE!_** Focused on God's plan and determined to not stop pushing until it has materialized.

In addition, it does not matter what has happen in our past. What happened then is what happened then. We must not allow the situations from our past to keep us from focusing on our future. This is exactly what Paul is saying in Philippians 3:13. The scripture reads "No, dear brothers and sisters, I have not achieved it, but I focus on this one thing: Forgetting the past and looking forward to what lies ahead..." (New Living Translation) This is a powerful verse and it is filled with so much truth. Paul is saying that he recognizes that he has not reached the place that he wants to be spiritually; but he will not allow the things that he did in his past to stop him from looking to what is in front of him. Now this is a really big statement for Paul to make because Paul experienced great success in his works for the church, but he also experienced much failure in his persecution of the church prior to his encounter with Jesus as well. In verse 13 Paul is saying it does not matter if he had a band of people celebrating his successes or attempting to crucify him for his failures he was not going to allow anything to prevent him from completing his work for Christ. Paul was clear when he said that his only responsibility was to focus on what was ahead of him and give no consideration to what was in his past.

In the same respect, we too must position ourselves as Paul did in Philippians 3:13 and **_BE!_** Focused on what lies ahead. I understand that many of us have had great success in our lives. As a result, we are now hovering around the water cooler of that success never moving from it in fear that there is no way for us to accomplish anything greater. On the other hand, many of us have experienced so much failure that we fear moving forward because we do not want to face that anguish of defeat again. Moreover, others of us are standing still because we have no clue what to do with our lives at this time. Please know that it does not matter which category you may fall into right now. What is required in this moment is that we begin to do as Isaiah did in Isaiah 50:7 when he said "Because the Sovereign Lord helps me, I will not be disgraced. Therefore, I have set my face like a stone, determined to do his will. And I know that I will not be put to shame." (New Living Translation) Here the scripture is saying that Isaiah was determined to stay focused on God's plan and will for his life regardless to what was happening around him. Isaiah knew that if he continued to focus on the Lord that he would not have to worry about being embarrassed because God would cover and protect him; and we must believe this as well. All we have to do is focus on the plan of God for our lives and trust that He will make our next steps prosperous. For this reason, let us make a conscious effort to **_BE!_** Focused on our future because God has a great work for us to complete for Him.

Prayer Starter

As you are praying and meditating today, ask God to help you to **_BE!_** Focused on the things that He has for you to do now and in your future. Ask Him to give you strength to release your past and move forward into the destiny He has ordained for your life. Ask God to remove every hindrance that is blocking you from accomplishing His plan for your life. Ask Him to reveal to you His plan for your life. Ask God to help you to push past your place of procrastination and move forward towards your next assignment. Ask Him to cover you as you seek to set your face like a stone that is fixed toward what is next for your life.

Scripture References

Philippians 3:13 (New Living Translation)
Isaiah 50:7 (New Living Translation)

Study Notes:

_BE!_ Focused

Day Twenty-Seven

BE! Prayerful

I was raised in the church and at fifteen years old I accepted Jesus as Lord and Savior over my life. This means that I am almost 100% positive that I know all of the church lingo and phraseology that is spoken in and out of houses of worship throughout the world (maybe a little exaggeration here). A good example of church lingo is when you tell someone to "be blessed" or you say to them in answer to their question "I'm blessed and highly favored." Another example is when the presider of a worship service says "God is good all the time" and the congregants respond "And, all the time God is good." I am confident that I know each and every phrase. As a matter of fact, there is one phrase that my mom would use all of the time and it took me a while to understand and appreciate the truth that rested within the words. Now that I have more life experience underneath my belt and a clearer perspective on life as well, I totally understand what my mom was saying. She would say to me "daughter I am going to *BE!* Prayerful" and she would remind me to do the same. It did not matter what I was going through or what I was faced with in life she would remind me to *BE!* Prayerful. When I was in the midst of deciding which undergraduate college I would attend or businesses that I would pursue she would simply tell me to *BE!* Prayerful. After hearing her say it for over half of my life I must admit that sometimes I would get a little upset at her answer. This is especially true in times when I really wanted her to give me an answer regarding something that I was going through that was opposite her normal response. I would get so frustrated because I wanted her to not give me a spiritual answer, but to instead hit me with all of her life's wisdom, knowledge and understanding. I wanted her to bypass the "God stuff" and tell me the "real deal." As a result, there were times when I would say "Ma, just tell me what you feel about the situation." But, she would look at me and say "I don't know daughter. All I know to do is pray." As I have grown in my relationship with God I now know what my mom was talking about. I truly understand why she would not make any moves without talking to God first. It is perfectly clear to me now that we must **BE!** Prayerful about everything that we do and say. My mom's utter and total dependence on God to lead and guide her in every area of her life served as an example for me and many others to follow. We must lean on God and trust that as we spend time with Him in prayer that He is going to lead us in the ways that we should take.

Further, this truth is expressed in Psalm 37:23. The verse reads "A person's steps are established by the Lord, and He takes pleasure in his way." (Christian Standard Bible) Here, the words "establish" means to make firm and "in his way" means journey. The verse is saying not only has God ordered or firmed up every step that we take; but He also finds pleasure in the journey that He planned for us. As a result, my mom had it completely right when she said she did not have answers for me other than that she would

197

pray. The answers to my questions were not locked up in the life experiences of my mom; but they were instead hidden in the mind of God. Therefore, the only way for me to get to the answers that I was seeking was through prayer; and as it was with me then it is the same for us right now. We must pray before we make any moves. God is the only one that knows our next steps because He is the one that designed and plotted out our lives. We have to spend time with Him to know what we are supposed to be doing today and the next days after.

In addition, the bible tells us in I Thessalonians 5:17 that we must pray without ceasing. If we follow this scripture we will always have a prayer of some kind flowing through our lips. These prayers may vary in length, but each will be purposeful and hold different significance and meaning. For instance, praying for a loved with cancer is a prayer that may be filled with urgency and in some cases desperation; but praying for a new car may have a different tone altogether. Either way, we should be in continuous communication with God. We should make every effort to say to ourselves what my mom said to me which is "I don't know… All I can do is pray." The same goes for when other people ask us about our lives and demand that we give them an answer. We should say to them that in and of ourselves we do not have an answer; but we are praying to the one who knows, sees, and can do everything. His plan for our lives has already been established; and we are just waiting to receive direction from Him.

Prayer Starter

As you are praying and meditating today, write down all of the decisions you have to make, issues, situations and problems that you may be facing; and then take all of it to God in prayer. Ask God to show you how to **_BE!_** Prayerful. Ask Him to give you wisdom concerning your relationships, job choices, house purchases and every other situation you are experiencing. Ask Him to give you the words to say as you seek to pray without ceasing until you get an answer from Him. Ask God to give you the strength to wait on Him and not take any steps until He has given you the direction you need.

Scripture References

Psalm 37:23 (Christian Standard Bible)
I Thessalonians 5:17

BE! Prayerful

Day Twenty-Eight

BE! Steadfast

I find it very interesting that as long as we are doing nothing special with our lives it seems as if the sun shines every day. We love everyone and they love us back; and all that is good in the world flows freely in and out of our lives. It really does seem like the world is on our side. This of course is the case until we make a decision to follow after our God-ordained purpose for life. When we make a hard turn and begin to focus on His will and plan it appears as if our enemy's camp receives a personal text warning them that we have awakened and are on assignment! When this occurs it may feel like the whole world instead of being for us has now shifted against us. The friends that were there for us when we were at our lowest point may have virtually disappeared. The family that we thought would always be by our sides may now be pulling away. The job that we love and have always received glowing accolades on our reviews is suddenly not pleased with any of our work. It really does look like as soon as we said yes to God that something changed and we are now faced with a new reality that has us feeling isolated and alone. My sister and my brother, if this is where you are today allow me to encourage you by saying that you are on the right track and in the right place. Whenever we begin to make adjustments in life that speak to positive and empowering changes we will interrupt the flow of the negative, dark and destructive powers that exist in the world. We have to know that this act of affecting change is never tolerated by our enemy and it will be challenged every time. I have discovered that the resistance we encounter will manifest in many forms; but it is most often launched out of relationships that are the closest to us. For this reason, we may find it difficult to continue pushing through to our destiny. As a result, I write the devotional for today to encourage each of us to **_BE!_** Steadfast in the things that God is leading us to do. Do not stop moving forward because everything will ultimately work out for our benefit in the end.

In I Corinthians 15:58 the bible says "Therefore, my dear brothers and sisters, be steadfast, immovable, always excelling in the Lord's work, because you know that your labor in the Lord is not in vain." (Christian Standard Bible) Other translations replace the world steadfast with firm or unshaken; while others proclaim that we should not allow ourselves to be moved off of our foundations. I actually love each of these because the verse of scripture is letting us know that we will be tested on what we say God has told us to do for Him. We know from the reading of this verse that we will not go dancing off into the sunset doing God's work without being challenged on our journey. At some point on our paths to accomplishing God's plan we will face adversity of some kind. It is our responsibility to know that this will occur and be prepared for the fall-out when it does. What this means to us is we must remain resolute or unwavering in our pursuit of God's purpose. We must not allow ourselves to become distracted from the call of God for any reason. We have to **_BE!_** Steadfast in the things of God. We must plant our feet firmly in the ground and be determined to accomplish His will for us regardless to all opposition.

In the same respect, I understand that what I am purposing may be easier said than done. This is because in many instances the person opposing the plan of God for our lives is a close family member or friend; and when they are not favorable to His plan, we experience emotions that are sometimes difficult to deal with and fight through. This is because we all expect that our family and friends are going to support us in everything that we do; but unfortunately this is not reality all of the time. Therefore, we are seemingly caught between moving forward with God and staying where we are with our loved ones; and the choice is not always easy.

Further, as a word of caution and from a place of love, let us not assume that the reaction of our family and friends is as of a result of "hateration." Many times the reason for our loved ones refusal to support us is not rooted in jealousy, envy or any such thing. Sometimes it is as a result of them being fearful of us getting hurt or making a mistake. They do not want to see us fall or experience embarrassment as a result of our decision to do something that they have never and will never do or in some cases even care to understand. Though there may be others that fall in the category of pure hate of us as we do things that they want to do but will not, we cannot afford to let either position stop us from succeeding at what God has already prepared a way for us to accomplish. We have to remain firm in our desire to get to where we have been designed to be before the foundations of the world. We cannot allow others to cause us to quit or give up our future for any reason. We must accomplish God's plan even at the cost of losing the ones that we love for a season and maybe even for a lifetime. If we ultimately want to hear God say to us "well done" we have no other option than to **_BE!_** Steadfast.

Prayer Starter

As you are praying and meditating today, ask God to help you to **_BE!_** Steadfast. Ask Him to help you to hear his voice over all of the negative voices that will shout to you what you cannot and should not do. Ask God to keep you in a place of love with all people even when they are showing you nothing but hate. Ask Him to plant your feet in the ground that you remain firm in the things that He is leading you to accomplish. Ask God to help you to not allow anyone to push you off of your foundation, but to give you the strength to complete the journey as He has ordained and predestined.

Scripture Reference

I Corinthians 15:58 (Christian Standard Bible)

_BE!_ Steadfast

Day Twenty-Nine

BE! Vulnerable

One of the most difficult things for us to do in life is to *BE!* Vulnerable. Vulnerability comes with great risk and not many of us are willing to expose ourselves to the negative effects that we may experience as a result. This is why in dating relationships neither party wants to be the first to say I love you. There is a lot of stress and anxiety involved in stepping out in the deep waters of love and expressing how one feels not knowing if those feelings will be reciprocated or not. In addition, pitching an idea to people needed to assist with or invest financially in a business can be overwhelming. It does not matter if the individuals are family or even friends. The process can be extremely emotional because once the idea is exposed to others the owner of it has no control over how it will be received or if it will be met with immediate rejection. For this reason, the risk that is involved in being vulnerable proves to sometimes be too great to endure. No one wants to be disappointed. Therefore, many of us are choosing to hold on to our fabulous and amazing ideas in fear of them not being accepted and having to deal with the feelings of rejection as a result.

Although a valid concern for being disappointed as a result of taking a risk exists being vulnerable does come with reward as well. Therefore, let us not stop the conversation at the expectation of rejection and explore the other side of the vulnerability coin where risk and reward reside together in harmony. In this moment, take time to consider every successful person in the world of social media today. Do not think about the A-list stars that are on television, film or stage. Just consider the Facebook, Twitter, Instagram and YouTube stars that are now millionaires because they took a step out of what was comfortable and launched out into the unknown. Yes, the move was risky; but the act has paid dividends that are undeniable for these individuals. Now, consider the ideas and dreams that are waiting to be brought to the market by you. What is holding you? What is stopping you? Is it fear of being rejected? Is it the risk of vulnerability that is preventing you from moving forward? If it is, think about all of the successful people in the world today. Let your mind roam across all areas of life and business and then consider the fact that not one of them got where they are right now without being vulnerable and taking risks. Ask yourself, how important it is for you to see this goal, dream or vision manifested. Then ask yourself if it is worth it for you to **_BE!_** Vulnerable that the world may be exposed to the beauty that you have to offer.

The idea of vulnerability is one that is seen in the Book of Esther and I encourage you to read all ten chapters to understand the story in its entirety. In this book of the bible, Esther, a Jewish woman was chosen as queen to a Persian King. At some point in the story one of the King's chief servants decided that he would kill all of the Jewish people. Esther, as Queen and a woman of Jewish decent was admonished to talk to the King on the behalf of her people to save them from death. Esther was fearful because no one could enter the presence of the King without being invited. To do so could mean sudden death. As a result, Esther was faced with a decision that meant she would be choosing between her life and her death. Esther was literally being asked to _**BE!**_ Vulnerable which meant that she made herself susceptible to either physical or emotional harm. Esther had a very difficult decision to make because the risk that she would be taking could prove to be deadly. Esther ultimately made the decision to go to the King unannounced to seek his intervention. The King allowed Esther to come into the inner court and he did as she asks and saved the lives of her people.

Now, please consider the fact that though entering into an unknown environment is intimidating and risky it is safe to say that the majority of us are not in a position where we may die if we stepped into a boardroom to pitch an idea or post a video of our business or ministry on Facebook. We may experience a lot of anxiety as a result, but for the majority of us death is more than likely not a worry. On the other hand, it was a real concern for Esther; but she did not let the risk stop her from doing what was necessary to save the Jewish people.

As it was for Esther, it must be the same for each of us as well. We cannot allow the fear of being vulnerable to prevent us from doing what is necessary for our success in life. We have to find the courage to move forward into what God has placed within us to accomplish. We must allow ourselves to _**BE!**_ Vulnerable and go after and accomplish the plans that are in our hearts. The deliverance that we need, the people that we need, the finances that we need are all on the other side of vulnerability. We must take the step, calculate the risk and move. Our best life is waiting for us.

Prayer Starter

As you are praying and meditating today, ask God to help you to *BE!* Vulnerable. Ask Him to help you to understand that there is risk in reward; that they both go hand in hand. Ask God to give you the strength to push past the expectation of the negative to receive the reward of the positive. As Esther did, Ask God to give you the boldness that you need to walk up to doors that are available for you, but you may not have been called to enter as of yet. Ask God to help you push past disappointment when it comes and continue to move forward into what He has designed for your life.

Scripture Reference

The Book of Esther

BE! Vulnerable

Day Thirty

BE! Light

When I think about the devotional for today I think about how many people live in darkness every day. This darkness may be literal because someone is impoverished and unable to pay their utility bill in order to receive electricity into their homes. In addition, the darkness may also be as a result of a lack of knowledge and understanding; whereby a person may be unable to comprehend a matter being discussed. Moreover, darkness may also be associated with a spiritual matter in which someone is living a life absent of the light of the word of God that provides us with clarity when we are in spiritually dark places. There are so many areas of life where darkness dwells that it is important for Christians to *BE!* Light in every dark place in the world.

In considering the word "light" and its application to multiple areas of life I am challenged to respond to the call to *BE!* Light. As this is the case, the question that I must ask myself is in what way am I supposed to impact the world with the light that is me; and I am hopeful that you are challenged and questioning yourself in the same way as well. In this moment in time, we must begin to inquire of ourselves the who, what, when, where and how of life. We must ask ourselves the question "as light where are we supposed to be in the world to impact the darkness; and what are we supposed to do to impact it when we get there." I must admit that this is where I am right now in my life. I say this because as soon as I became settled and happy with where I was with my educational and career goals, I started to feel a pull to do more. It was really interesting because I was ready to settle into my new life and bask in my accomplishments; but the Lord would not allow me to do so. I kept being pulled towards an assignment that I thought I had completed years ago. It was not until I submitted to God and said yes that I began to understand that I had not even scratched the surface of what God had said I should do. I had not begun to affect the darkness that God had called me to interrupt. It is imperative that we understand our obligation to make a difference in this world and **_BE!_** Light in dark situations that we have been gifted and anointed to impact for the Kingdom of God. We have been called for this purpose and we must complete our assignments as mandated to us by God.

The bible says in Matthew 5:14-16 that:

> You are the light of the world. A city situated on a hill cannot be hidden. No one lights a lamp and puts it under a basket, but rather on a lampstand, and it gives light for all who are in the house. In the same way, let your light shine before others, so that they may see your good works and give glory to your Father in heaven. (Christian Standard Version)

218

Here, the word light is defined to mean the natural agent that stimulates sight and makes things visible. In this verse of scripture, Jesus is saying to us that it is natural for us to **_BE!_** Light. It is not something that we have to work hard at doing because it is naturally who we are. As such, we have the ability to help the world to see things that they could not see before. As a matter of fact, we naturally shine so bright that we are able to impact the people in this entire world as light thereby illuminating the vision, wisdom and understanding of all that we reach. Therefore, we must be careful that we not dim our lights because other people think we are shinning too bright. It is in our nature to illuminate dark places that people are positively affected and transformed. We ultimately want those that we are accountable to shining our light upon to see God in us and glorify Him for the light that they have experienced as a result of our obedience.

It is for this reason that we must seek God for direction as it relates to the dark places that we are assigned to as light. What has God gifted and anointed you to do or to be? Where has He been pulling you to go but you keep saying no? Have you been called to the marketplace to work? Has God gifted you to speak to nations? Do you feel a pull to teach children? What has He told you years ago to do, but you have refused to step into it for reasons that may be justifiable; but are still not enough to have God change his mind about you fulfilling His plan. We must understand that there are lives at stake. When we do not enter into the areas that we have been called we are impacting not only ourselves but the people who we are assigned to us as well. Light is the only thing that can dispel darkness. We have to make a decision today to **_BE!_** Light in the areas in which we have been called. There are many people trapped in dark places and they need us to be able see clearly and walk out of what has been holding them for years. As a result, let us make a decision today to **_BE!_** Light to this world that our Father will be glorified in heaven.

Prayer Starter

As you are praying and meditating today, ask God to help you to **_BE!_** Light in this world of darkness. Ask Him to show you where He has called you to be and what He has called you to do that you will begin to affect change in the areas that you have been assigned. Ask God to help you to shine so bright that the people around you will be unable to deny that He lives within you. Ask Him to help you to not diminish the light that you are for the benefit others. Ask God to help you to always be reminded that you are light and that the world needs you.

Scripture Reference

Matthew 5:14-16 (Christian Standard Version)

BE! Light

_____
_____
_____
_____
_____
_____
_____
_____
_____
_____
_____
_____
_____
_____
_____
_____
_____
_____
_____
_____
_____
_____
_____
_____
_____
_____
_____
_____
_____
_____
_____
_____
_____

Day Thirty-One

BE! An Experience

I was watching something on television not too long ago and heard someone say something that touched me at the very core of my being. She said that not only is the life that she lives an experience, but she in and of herself is an experience as well. When I heard her say that it first of all coincided with an event idea that God has given me for women; but it also challenged the way that I think about what I do on a daily basis and what type of experiences I may be having in my everyday life. Have you ever stopped to consider the experiences you are having as you do chores, drive your car, eat, shop for groceries or even the ones you are having at work. If I have, I can assure you that it has not be a conscious thought; but more than likely a passing and also fading one that I cannot even remember. When I heard her make that statement I concluded in that very moment that I was going to make everything that I do from that point forward an experience. I decided that I would no longer live a mundane existence. It was time to put some color back into my life and start enjoying every aspect of life; but it was also time to leave my mark in this life as well.

As a result, I decided that when people encounter me that they will have an experience with me that is like no other. What do I mean by this statement you may ask? Well, it's simple. Think about the worse customer service experience you have ever had in your life. How did it make you feel? Who did you talk to about your experience afterwards? How long afterwards did you talk about the experience? Were you upset enough to write a negative review on Yelp? Now, think about the reverse of that situation. The same amount of energy that you may have put into complaining and discussing your negative experience is the same amount of energy that I want people to put into talking about their incredibly positive experience with me. I want them to feel my energy for days to come after we have departed ways. I want to impact the lives of people in such a way that my disposition causes them to want to display the same joy and energy that I demonstrated in their lives as well. Come join me on my journey as I endeavor to **_BE!_** An Experience for myself and for all that I encounter. We can show the world how to live life in such a way that we leave positive impressions in the hearts of every person that we meet.

Further, we should take note that the desire to **_BE!_** An Experience falls right in line with the will of God for our lives. There are many accounts of Jesus being an experience and positively impacting lives of men and women throughout the bible. For example, He healed the nobleman's son in John 4:46-54, He healed the paralyzed man at the pool of Bethesda in John 5:1-15, He fed 5000 people in John 6:5-14, He healed the man who was blind from the time of birth in John 9:1-7, He raised Lazarus from the dead in John 11:1-44, and performed many other miracles that we do not have enough time to discuss. Jesus was an experience because everybody that He touched left His presence changed. Each person experienced Jesus in such a way that it was undeniable that they had spent time with Him.

Therefore, as it was with Jesus, it should also be the same way with us. We should make every attempt to infect people with the love and joy that radiates through us as followers of Christ. When people leave our presence we should be assured that if they had to come back to us to discuss anything at all that they not only can, but will because of their prior experiences with us. Our co-workers should look forward to seeing us every day at work because we have a positive impact on their lives; and our families should be waiting at the door for us when we arrive home because they long to be in our presence. In addition, we should seek to **_BE!_** An Experience not only in the presence of people that we know, but those that we do not know as well. Our goal should be to make a difference in this world in such a way that we are memorable individually, but Jesus is recognized ultimately. Our main objective should always be for us to be great examples of who Jesus is here on the earth.

For these reasons, let us make the decision today that we are going to **_BE!_** An Experience. Declare that every person that you come into contact with will leave your presence having had a positive encounter with you that they will remember for many days after. Let us endeavor to be like Jesus that the love and compassion that He showed people will illuminate out of us and attach itself to the hearts of everyone that we meet.

Prayer Starter

As you are praying and meditating today, ask God to help you to **_BE!_** An Experience. Ask Him to show you how to make a positive impact on all that you encounter. Ask God to help you to always be aware of what you are saying to others and how you are saying it remembering that you represent Him at all times. Ask Him to give you wisdom in your approach as you seek to create positive experiences for every person that comes into your presences.

Scripture References

John 4:46-54
John 5:1-15
John 6:5-14
John 9:1-7
John 11:1-44

BE! An Experience

_____
_____
_____
_____
_____
_____
_____
_____
_____
_____
_____
_____
_____
_____
_____
_____
_____
_____
_____
_____
_____
_____
_____
_____
_____
_____
_____
_____
_____
_____
_____
_____
_____
_____

About The Author

A native of New Orleans, Louisiana, Teta is a licensed Minister who has preached the gospel of Jesus Christ over twenty-five years. Her first message, "Kill the spider: Dealing with your past before it destroys your present and your future" ushered her into a ministry that has blessed the lives of many across the United States.

Teta has a passion for people; and desires for everyone to live a life of absolute wholeness. To that end, she analogizes that as a doctor is commissioned to address the ailments of our physical bodies, so is she called to administer healing to our hearts, our souls and our minds.

She is a worshipper at heart who knows that the presence of God is her safe place. As she pours out her love upon God and God in turn pours out His love upon her, Teta confidently ministers the word of God in power that lives are transformed; never to be the same again.

Teta is the Founder and Managing/Member of Empowering To Be, LLC, an Attorney, an Entrepreneur, a Possibilities Coach and a Mentor to many. Her goal in life is to motivate and encourage women of all ages to go after "it" – whatever "it" is... because as long as you are still living... it is NEVER too late to accomplish your dream.

Thank You

Thank you to my family and to my friends that have labored with me to bring the vision of God to pass. I do not have the words to express how much I love and appreciate you. Let's go see what God has in store for us. Our Next is Now!

Smooches!
Teta J.